Cram101 Textbook Outlines to accompany:

Theories of Personality: Understanding Persons

Cloninger, 4th Edition

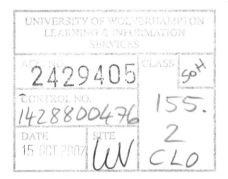
An Academic Internet Publishers (AIPI) publication (c) 2007.

You have a discounted membership at www.Cram101.com with this book.

Get all of the practice tests for the chapters of this textbook, and access in-depth reference material for writing essays and papers. Here is an example from a Cram101 Biology text:

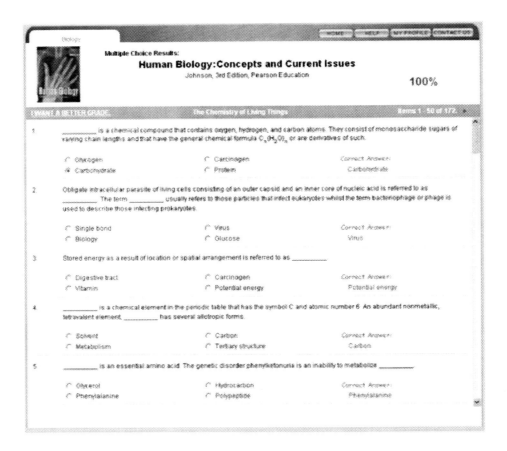

When you need problem solving help with math, stats, and other disciplines, www.Cram101.com will walk through the formulas and solutions step by step.

With Cram101.com online, you also have access to extensive reference material.

You will nail those essays and papers. Here is an example from a Cram101 Biology text:

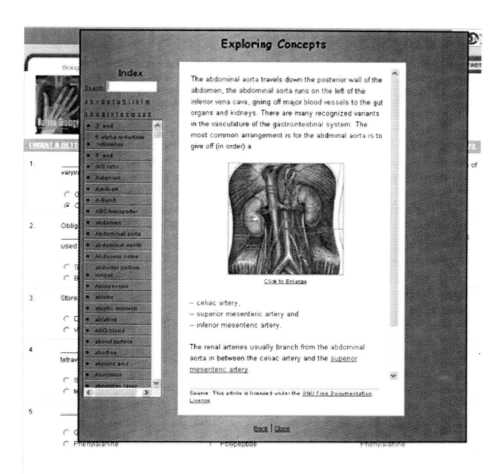

Visit **www.Cram101.com**, click Sign Up at the top of the screen, and enter DK73DW in the promo code box on the registration screen. Access to www.Cram101.com is normally $9.95, but because you have purchased this book, your access fee is only $4.95. Sign up and stop highlighting textbooks forever.

Learning System

Cram101 Textbook Outlines is a learning system. The notes in this book are the highlights of your textbook, you will never have to highlight a book again.

How to use this book. Take this book to class, it is your notebook for the lecture. The notes and highlights on the left hand side of the pages follow the outline and order of the textbook. All you have to do is follow along while your intructor presents the lecture. Circle the items emphasized in class and add other important information on the right side. With Cram101 Textbook Outlines you'll spend less time writing and more time listening. Learning becomes more efficient.

Cram101.com Online

Increase your studying efficiency by using Cram101.com's practice tests and online reference material. It is the perfect complement to Cram101 Textbook Outlines. Use self-teaching matching tests or simulate in-class testing with comprehensive multiple choice tests, or simply use Cram's true and false tests for quick review. Cram101.com even allows you to enter your in-class notes for an integrated studying format combining the textbook notes with your class notes.

Theories of Personality: Understanding Persons
Cloninger, 4th

CONTENTS

Human nature	Human nature is the fundamental nature and substance of humans, as well as the range of human behavior that is believed to be invariant over long periods of time and across very different cultural contexts.
Motivation	In psychology, motivation is the driving force (desire) behind all actions of an organism.
Emotion	An emotion is a mental states that arise spontaneously, rather than through conscious effort. They are often accompanied by physiological changes.
Personality	Personality refers to the pattern of enduring characteristics that differentiates a person, the patterns of behaviors that make each individual unique.
Theories	Theories are logically self-consistent models or frameworks describing the behavior of a certain natural or social phenomenon. They are broad explanations and predictions concerning phenomena of interest.
Individual differences	Individual differences psychology studies the ways in which individual people differ in their behavior. This is distinguished from other aspects of psychology in that although psychology is ostensibly a study of individuals, modern psychologists invariably study groups.
Trait	An enduring personality characteristic that tends to lead to certain behaviors is called a trait. The term trait also means a genetically inherited feature of an organism.
Personality type	A persistent style of complex behaviors defined by a group of related traits is referred to as a personality type. Myer Friedman and his co-workers first defined personality types in the 1950s. Friedman classified people into 2 categories, Type A and Type B.
Personality trait	According to the Diagnostic and Statistical Manual of the American Psychiatric Association, a personality trait is a "prominent aspect of personality that is exhibited in a wide range of important social and personal contexts. ...".
Correlation	A statistical technique for determining the degree of association between two or more variables is referred to as correlation.
Quantitative	A quantitative property is one that exists in a range of magnitudes, and can therefore be measured. Measurements of any particular quantitative property are expressed as as a specific quantity, referred to as a unit, multiplied by a number.
Variable	A variable refers to a measurable factor, characteristic, or attribute of an individual or a system.
Personality test	A personality test aims to describe aspects of a person's character that remain stable across situations.
Nomothetic	Nomothetic measures are contrasted to ipsative or idiothetic measures, where nomothetic measures are measures that can be taken directly by an outside observer, such as weight or how many times a particular behavior occurs, and ipsative measures are self-reports such as a rank-ordered list of preferences.
Idiographic	An idiographic investigation studies the characteristics of an individual in depth.
Population	Population refers to all members of a well-defined group of organisms, events, or things.
Sears	Sears focused on the application of the social learning theory (SLT) to socialization processes, and how children internalize the values, attitudes, and behaviors predominant in their culture. He articulated the place of parents in fostering internalization. In addition, he was among the first social learning theorists to officially acknowledge the reciprocal interaction on an individual's behavior and their environment
Case study	A carefully drawn biography that may be obtained through interviews, questionnaires, and psychological tests is called a case study.
Personality psychology	Personality psychology is a branch of psychology which studies personality and individual difference processes. One emphasis in personality psychology is on trying to create a coherent picture of a person

and all his or her major psychological processes.

Positive relationship	Statistically, a positive relationship refers to a mathematical relationship in which increases in one measure are matched by increases in the other.
Attention	Attention is the cognitive process of selectively concentrating on one thing while ignoring other things. Psychologists have labeled three types of attention: sustained attention, selective attention, and divided attention.
Sigmund Freud	Sigmund Freud was the founder of the psychoanalytic school, based on his theory that unconscious motives control much behavior, that particular kinds of unconscious thoughts and memories are the source of neurosis, and that neurosis could be treated through bringing these unconscious thoughts and memories to consciousness in psychoanalytic treatment.
Carl Rogers	Carl Rogers was instrumental in the development of non-directive psychotherapy, also known as "client-centered" psychotherapy. Rogers' basic tenets were unconditional positive regard, genuineness, and empathic understanding, with each demonstrated by the counselor.
Adaptation	Adaptation is a lowering of sensitivity to a stimulus following prolonged exposure to that stimulus. Behavioral adaptations are special ways a particular organism behaves to survive in its natural habitat.
Psychoanalytic theory	Psychoanalytic theory is a general term for approaches to psychoanalysis which attempt to provide a conceptual framework more-or-less independent of clinical practice rather than based on empirical analysis of clinical cases.
Psychoanalytic	Freud's theory that unconscious forces act as determinants of personality is called psychoanalytic theory. The theory is a developmental theory characterized by critical stages of development.
Society	The social sciences use the term society to mean a group of people that form a semi-closed (or semi-open) social system, in which most interactions are with other individuals belonging to the group.
Temperament	Temperament refers to a basic, innate disposition to change behavior. The activity level is an important dimension of temperament.
Infancy	The developmental period that extends from birth to 18 or 24 months is called infancy.
Developmental psychologist	A psychologist interested in human growth and development from conception until death is referred to as a developmental psychologist.
Biological predisposition	The genetic readiness of animals and humans to perform certain behaviors is a biological predisposition.
Predisposition	Predisposition refers to an inclination or diathesis to respond in a certain way, either inborn or acquired. In abnormal psychology, it is a factor that lowers the ability to withstand stress and inclines the individual toward pathology.
Kagan	The work of Kagan supports the concept of an inborn, biologically based temperamental predisposition to severe anxiety.
Heredity	Heredity is the transfer of characteristics from parent to offspring through their genes.
Neuroscience	A field that combines the work of psychologists, biologists, biochemists, medical researchers, and others in the study of the structure and function of the nervous system is neuroscience.
Genetics	Genetics is the science of genes, heredity, and the variation of organisms.
Learning	Learning is a relatively permanent change in behavior that results from experience. Thus, to attribute a behavioral change to learning, the change must be relatively permanent and must result from experience.
Attachment	Attachment is the tendency to seek closeness to another person and feel secure when that person is

Go to **Cram101.com** for the Practice Tests for this Chapter.

present.

Operational definition	An operational definition is the definition of a concept or action in terms of the observable and repeatable process, procedures, and appartaus that illustrates the concept or action.
Scientific method	Psychologists gather data in order to describe, understand, predict, and control behavior. Scientific method refers to an approach that can be used to discover accurate information. It includes these steps: understand the problem, collect data, draw conclusions, and revise research conclusions.
Self-esteem	Self-esteem refers to a person's subjective appraisal of himself or herself as intrinsically positive or negative to some degree.
Determinism	Determinism is the philosophical proposition that every event, including human cognition and action, is causally determined by an unbroken chain of prior occurrences.
Empirical	Empirical means the use of working hypotheses which are capable of being disproved using observation or experiment.
Construct	A generalized concept, such as anxiety or gravity, is a construct.
Hypothesis	A specific statement about behavior or mental processes that is testable through research is a hypothesis.
Control group	A group that does not receive the treatment effect in an experiment is referred to as the control group or sometimes as the comparison group.
Free will	The idea that human beings are capable of freely making choices or decisions is free will.
Self-image	A person's self-image is the mental picture, generally of a kind that is quite resistant to change, that depicts not only details that are potentially available to objective investigation by others, but also items that have been learned by that person about himself or herself.
Applied research	Applied research is done to solve specific, practical questions; its primary aim is not to gain knowledge for its own sake. It can be exploratory but often it is descriptive. It is almost always done on the basis of basic research.
Basic research	Basic research has as its primary objective the advancement of knowledge and the theoretical understanding of the relations among variables . It is exploratory and often driven by the researcher's curiosity, interest or hunch.
Heuristic	A heuristic is a simple, efficient rule of thumb proposed to explain how people make decisions, come to judgments and solve problems, typically when facing complex problems or incomplete information. These rules work well under most circumstances, but in certain cases lead to systematic cognitive biases.
Deductive reasoning	Deductive reasoning refers to a form of reasoning about arguments in which conclusions are determined from the premises. The conclusions are true if the premises are true.
Reasoning	Reasoning is the act of using reason to derive a conclusion from certain premises. There are two main methods to reach a conclusion,deductive reasoning and inductive reasoning.
Research method	The scope of the research method is to produce some new knowledge. This, in principle, can take three main forms: Exploratory research; Constructive research; and Empirical research.
Questionnaire	A self-report method of data collection or clinical assessment method in which the individual being studied checks off items on a printed list, answers multiple-choice questions, or writes out answers to essay questions aimed at producing a selfdescription is called questionnaire.
Immune system	The most important function of the human immune system occurs at the cellular level of the blood and tissues. The lymphatic and blood circulation systems are highways for specialized white blood cells. These cells include B cells, T cells, natural killer cells, and macrophages. All function with the primary objective of recognizing, attacking and destroying bacteria, viruses, cancer cells, and all substances seen as foreign.

Reliability	Reliability means the extent to which a test produces a consistent , reproducible score .
Test-retest reliability	The consistency of a measure when it is repeated over time is called test-retest reliability. It involves administering the test to the same group of people at least twice. The first set of scores is correlated with the second set of scores. Correlations range between 0 (low reliability) and 1 (high reliability).
Validity	The extent to which a test measures what it is intended to measure is called validity.
Predictive validity	Predictive validity refers to the relation between test scores and the student 's future performance .
Assertiveness	Assertiveness basically means the ability to express your thoughts and feelings in a way that clearly states your needs and keeps the lines of communication open with the other.
Anxiety	Anxiety is a complex combination of the feeling of fear, apprehension and worry often accompanied by physical sensations such as palpitations, chest pain and/or shortness of breath.
Construct validity	The extent to which there is evidence that a test measures a particular hypothetical construct is referred to as construct validity.
Cronbach	Cronbach is most famous for the development of Cronbach's alpha, a method for determining the reliability of educational and psychological tests. His work on test reliability reached an acme with the creation of generalizability theory, a statistical model for identifying and quantifying the sources of measurement error.
Thematic Apperception Test	The Thematic Apperception Test uses a standard series of provocative yet ambiguous pictures about which the subject must tell a story. Each story is carefully analyzed to uncover underlying needs, attitudes, and patterns of reaction.
Projective test	A projective test is a personality test designed to let a person respond to ambiguous stimuli, presumably revealing hidden emotions and internal conflicts. This is different from an "objective test" in which responses are analyzed according to a universal standard rather than an individual psychiatrist's judgement.
Apperception	A newly experienced sensation is related to past experiences to form an understood situation. For Wundt, consciousness is composed of two "stages:" There is a large capacity working memory called the Blickfeld and the narrower consciousness called Apperception, or selective attention.
Rorschach	The Rorschach inkblot test is a method of psychological evaluation. It is a projective test associated with the Freudian school of thought. Psychologists use this test to try to probe the unconscious minds of their patients.
Psychological test	Psychological test refers to a standardized measure of a sample of a person's behavior.
Correlational research	Research that examines the relationship between two sets of variables to determine whether they are associated is called correlational research.
Causation	Causation concerns the time order relationship between two or more objects such that if a specific antecendent condition occurs the same consequent must always follow.
Social skills	Social skills are skills used to interact and communicate with others to assist status in the social structure and other motivations.
Independent variable	A condition in a scientific study that is manipulated (assigned different values by a researcher) so that the effects of the manipulation may be observed is called an independent variable.
Experimental group	Experimental group refers to any group receiving a treatment effect in an experiment.
Dependent	A measure of an assumed effect of an independent variable is called the dependent variable.

Go to **Cram101.com** for the Practice Tests for this Chapter.

variable	
Bandura	Bandura is best known for his work on social learning theory or Social Cognitivism. His famous Bobo doll experiment illustrated that people learn from observing others.
Mischel	Mischel is known for his cognitive social learning model of personality that focuses on the specific cognitive variables that mediate the manner in which new experiences affect the individual.
Psychodynamic	Most psychodynamic approaches are centered around the idea of a maladapted function developed early in life (usually childhood) which are at least in part unconscious. This maladapted function (a.k.a. defense mechanism) does not do well in place of a normal/healthy one.
Random assignment	Assignment of participants to experimental and control groups by chance is called random assignment. Random assigment reduces the likelihood that the results are due to preexisiting systematic differences between the groups.
Psychotherapy	Psychotherapy is a set of techniques based on psychological principles intended to improve mental health, emotional or behavioral issues.
Psychohistory	Psychohistory is the study of the psychological motivations of historical events. It combines the insights of psychotherapy with the research methodology of the social sciences to understand the emotional origin of the social and political behavior of groups and nations, past and present.
Insight	Insight refers to a sudden awareness of the relationships among various elements that had previously appeared to be independent of one another.
Adler	Adler argued that human personality could be explained teleologically, separate strands dominated by the guiding purpose of the individual's unconscious self ideal to convert feelings of inferiority to superiority (or rather completeness). The desires of the self ideal were countered by social and ethical demands.
Jung	Jung was in some aspects a response to Sigmund Freud's psychoanalysis. He proposed and developed the concepts of the extroverted and introverted personality, archetypes, and the collective unconscious. His work has been influential in psychiatry and in the study of religion, literature, and related fields.
Psychoanalysis	Psychoanalysis refers to the school of psychology that emphasizes the importance of unconscious motives and conflicts as determinants of human behavior. It was Freud's method of exploring human personality.
Transference	Transference is a phenomenon in psychology characterized by unconscious redirection of feelings from one person to another.
Humanistic psychology	Humanistic psychology refers to the school of psychology that focuses on the uniqueness of human beings and their capacity for choice, growth, and psychological health.
Humanistic	Humanistic refers to any system of thought focused on subjective experience and human problems and potentials.
Social influence	Social influence is when the actions or thoughts of individual(s) are changed by other individual(s). Peer pressure is an example of social influence.
Paradigm	Paradigm refers to the set of practices that defines a scientific discipline during a particular period of time. It provides a framework from which to conduct research, it ensures that a certain range of phenomena, those on which the paradigm focuses, are explored thoroughly. Itmay also blind scientists to other, perhaps more fruitful, ways of dealing with their subject matter.

Go to **Cram101.com** for the Practice Tests for this Chapter.
And, **NEVER** highlight a book again!

Psychoanalytic	Freud's theory that unconscious forces act as determinants of personality is called psychoanalytic theory. The theory is a developmental theory characterized by critical stages of development.
Personality	Personality refers to the pattern of enduring characteristics that differentiates a person, the patterns of behaviors that make each individual unique.
Self-understanding	Self-understanding is a child's cognitive representation of the self, the substance and content of the child's self-conceptions.
Theories	Theories are logically self-consistent models or frameworks describing the behavior of a certain natural or social phenomenon. They are broad explanations and predictions concerning phenomena of interest.
Psychoanalyst	A psychoanalyst is a specially trained therapist who attempts to treat the individual by uncovering and revealing to the individual otherwise subconscious factors that are contributing to some undesirable behavior.
Consciousness	The awareness of the sensations, thoughts, and feelings being experienced at a given moment is called consciousness.
Psychoanalysis	Psychoanalysis refers to the school of psychology that emphasizes the importance of unconscious motives and conflicts as determinants of human behavior. It was Freud's method of exploring human personality.
Psychotherapy	Psychotherapy is a set of techniques based on psychological principles intended to improve mental health, emotional or behavioral issues.
Defense mechanism	A Defense mechanism is a set of unconscious ways to protect one's personality from unpleasant thoughts and realities which may otherwise cause anxiety. The notion is an integral part of the psychoanalytic theory.
Repression	A defense mechanism, repression involves moving thoughts unacceptable to the ego into the unconscious, where they cannot be easily accessed.
Empirical	Empirical means the use of working hypotheses which are capable of being disproved using observation or experiment.
Sexual abuse	Sexual abuse is a term used to describe non- consentual sexual relations between two or more parties which are considered criminally and/or morally offensive.
Inference	Inference is the act or process of drawing a conclusion based solely on what one already knows.
Ambiguous stimuli	Patterns that allow more than one perceptual organization are called ambiguous stimuli.
Rorschach	The Rorschach inkblot test is a method of psychological evaluation. It is a projective test associated with the Freudian school of thought. Psychologists use this test to try to probe the unconscious minds of their patients.
Projective test	A projective test is a personality test designed to let a person respond to ambiguous stimuli, presumably revealing hidden emotions and internal conflicts. This is different from an "objective test" in which responses are analyzed according to a universal standard rather than an individual psychiatrist's judgement.
Population	Population refers to all members of a well-defined group of organisms, events, or things.
Psychoanalytic theory	Psychoanalytic theory is a general term for approaches to psychoanalysis which attempt to provide a conceptual framework more-or-less independent of clinical practice rather than based on empirical analysis of clinical cases.

Motivation	In psychology, motivation is the driving force (desire) behind all actions of an organism.
Operational definition	An operational definition is the definition of a concept or action in terms of the observable and repeatable process, procedures, and apparatus that illustrates the concept or action.
Construct	A generalized concept, such as anxiety or gravity, is a construct.
Sympathetic	The sympathetic nervous system activates what is often termed the "fight or flight response". It is an automatic regulation system, that is, one that operates without the intervention of conscious thought.
Instinct	Instinct is the word used to describe inherent dispositions towards particular actions. They are generally an inherited pattern of responses or reactions to certain kinds of situations.
Ego	In Freud's view the Ego serves to balance our primitive needs and our moral beliefs and taboos. Relying on experience, a healthy Ego provides the ability to adapt to reality and interact with the outside world.
Role model	A person who serves as a positive example of desirable behavior is referred to as a role model.
Analytical psychology	Analytical psychology is based upon the movement started by Carl Jung and his followers as distinct from Freudian psychoanalysis. Its aim is the personal experience of the deep forces and motivations underlying human behavior.
Jung	Jung was in some aspects a response to Sigmund Freud's psychoanalysis. He proposed and developed the concepts of the extroverted and introverted personality, archetypes, and the collective unconscious. His work has been influential in psychiatry and in the study of religion, literature, and related fields.
Self-worth	In psychology, self-esteem or self-worth refers to a person's subjective appraisal of himself or herself as intrinsically positive or negative to some degree.
Adler	Adler argued that human personality could be explained teleologically, separate strands dominated by the guiding purpose of the individual's unconscious self ideal to convert feelings of inferiority to superiority (or rather completeness). The desires of the self ideal were countered by social and ethical demands.
Trait	An enduring personality characteristic that tends to lead to certain behaviors is called a trait. The term trait also means a genetically inherited feature of an organism.
Five-factor theory	The five-factor theory of personality proposes that there are five universal dimensions of personality: Neuroticism, Extraversion, Openness, Conscientiousness, and Agreeableness.
Conscientiousness	Conscientiousness is one of the dimensions of the five-factor model of personality and individual differences involving being organized, thorough, and reliable as opposed to careless, negligent, and unreliable.
Learning	Learning is a relatively permanent change in behavior that results from experience. Thus, to attribute a behavioral change to learning, the change must be relatively permanent and must result from experience.
Individualist	A person who defines the self in terms of personal traits and gives priority to personal goals is an individualist.
Genitals	Genitals refers to the internal and external reproductive organs.
Cognitive learning	Higher-level learning involving thinking, knowing, understanding, and anticipation is cognitive learning.
Bandura	Bandura is best known for his work on social learning theory or Social Cognitivism. His famous Bobo doll experiment illustrated that people learn from observing others.

Go to Cram101.com for the Practice Tests for this Chapter.

Go to **Cram101.com** for the Practice Tests for this Chapter.
And, **NEVER** highlight a book again!

Society	The social sciences use the term society to mean a group of people that form a semi-closed (or semi-open) social system, in which most interactions are with other individuals belonging to the group.
Self-actualization	Self-actualization (a term originated by Kurt Goldstein) is the instinctual need of a human to make the most of their unique abilities. Maslow described it as follows: Self Actualization is the intrinsic growth of what is already in the organism, or more accurately, of what the organism is.
Libido	Sigmund Freud suggested that libido is the instinctual energy or force that can come into conflict with the conventions of civilized behavior. Jung, condidered the libido as the free creative, or psychic, energy an individual has to put toward personal development, or individuation.
Stages	Stages represent relatively discrete periods of time in which functioning is qualitatively different from functioning at other periods.
Suicide	Suicide behavior is rare in childhood but escalates in adolescence. The suicide rate increases in a linear fashion from adolescence through late adulthood.
Attention	Attention is the cognitive process of selectively concentrating on one thing while ignoring other things. Psychologists have labeled three types of attention: sustained attention, selective attention, and divided attention.
Self-esteem	Self-esteem refers to a person's subjective appraisal of himself or herself as intrinsically positive or negative to some degree.
Fixation	Fixation in abnormal psychology is the state where an individual becomes obsessed with an attachment to another human, animal or inanimate object. Fixation in vision refers to maintaining the gaze in a constant direction. .
Thanatos	In psychoanalytical theory, Thanatos is the death instinct, which opposes Eros. The "death instinct" identified by Sigmund Freud, which signals a desire to give up the struggle of life and return to quiescence and the grave.
Sublimation	Sublimation is a coping mechanism. It refers to rechanneling sexual or aggressive energy into pursuits that society considers acceptable or admirable.
Perception	Perception is the process of acquiring, interpreting, selecting, and organizing sensory information.
Denial	Denial is a psychological defense mechanism in which a person faced with a fact that is uncomfortable or painful to accept rejects it instead, insisting that it is not true despite what may be overwhelming evidence.
Social influence	Social influence is when the actions or thoughts of individual(s) are changed by other individual(s). Peer pressure is an example of social influence.
Homosexuality	Homosexuality refers to a sexual orientation characterized by aesthetic attraction, romantic love, and sexual desire exclusively for members of the same sex or gender identity.
Sigmund Freud	Sigmund Freud was the founder of the psychoanalytic school, based on his theory that unconscious motives control much behavior, that particular kinds of unconscious thoughts and memories are the source of neurosis, and that neurosis could be treated through bringing these unconscious thoughts and memories to consciousness in psychoanalytic treatment.
Species	Species refers to a reproductively isolated breeding population.
Darwin	Darwin achieved lasting fame as originator of the theory of evolution through natural selection. His book Expression of Emotions in Man and Animals is generally considered the first text on comparative psychology.

Go to **Cram101.com** for the Practice Tests for this Chapter.

Discrimination	In Learning theory, discrimination refers the ability to distinguish between a conditioned stimulus and other stimuli. It can be brought about by extensive training or differential reinforcement. In social terms, it is the denial of privileges to a person or a group on the basis of prejudice.
Psychological disorder	Mental processes and/or behavior patterns that cause emotional distress and/or substantial impairment in functioning is a psychological disorder.
Hysteria	Hysteria is a diagnostic label applied to a state of mind, one of unmanageable fear or emotional excesses. The fear is often centered on a body part, most often on an imagined problem with that body part.
Affect	A subjective feeling or emotional tone often accompanied by bodily expressions noticeable to others is called affect.
Psychiatrist	A psychiatrist is a physician who specializes in the diagnosis and treatment of psychological disorders.
Determinism	Determinism is the philosophical proposition that every event, including human cognition and action, is causally determined by an unbroken chain of prior occurrences.
Neurologist	A physician who studies the nervous system, especially its structure, functions, and abnormalities is referred to as neurologist.
Depression	In everyday language depression refers to any downturn in mood, which may be relatively transitory and perhaps due to something trivial. This is differentiated from Clinical depression which is marked by symptoms that last two weeks or more and are so severe that they interfere with daily living.
Anesthesia	Anesthesia is the process of blocking the perception of pain and other sensations. This allows patients to undergo surgery and other procedures without the distress and pain they would otherwise experience.
Sensation	Sensation is the first stage in the chain of biochemical and neurologic events that begins with the impinging of a stimulus upon the receptor cells of a sensory organ, which then leads to perception, the mental state that is reflected in statements like "I see a uniformly blue wall."
Anxiety	Anxiety is a complex combination of the feeling of fear, apprehension and worry often accompanied by physical sensations such as palpitations, chest pain and/or shortness of breath.
Neuron	The neuron is the primary cell of the nervous system. They are found in the brain, the spinal cord, in the nerves and ganglia of the peripheral nervous system. It is a specialized cell that conducts impulses through the nervous system and contains three major parts: cell body, dendrites, and an axon. It can have many dendrites but only one axon.
Brain	The brain controls and coordinates most movement, behavior and homeostatic body functions such as heartbeat, blood pressure, fluid balance and body temperature. Functions of the brain are responsible for cognition, emotion, memory, motor learning and other sorts of learning. The brain is primarily made up of two types of cells: glia and neurons.
Animal magnetism	Animal magnetism is both a synonym for Mesmerism as well as the 18th century term for the supposed ethereal medium postulated by Franz Mesmer as a therapeutic agent. Its existence was examined by a French royal commission in 1784, and the commission concluded there was no evidence of its existence.
Psychodynamic	Most psychodynamic approaches are centered around the idea of a maladapted function developed early in life (usually childhood) which are at least in part unconscious. This maladapted function (a.k.a. defense mechanism) does not do well in place of a normal/healthy one.

Hypnosis	Hypnosis is a psychological state whose existence and effects are strongly debated. Some believe that it is a state under which the subject's mind becomes so suggestible that the hypnotist, the one who induces the state, can establish communication with the subconscious mind of the subject and command behavior that the subject would not choose to perform in a conscious state.
Charcot	Charcot took an interest in the malady then called hysteria. It seemed to be a mental disorder with physical manifestations, of immediate interest to a neurologist. He believed that hysteria was the result of a weak neurological system which was hereditary.
Breuer	Breuer is perhaps best known for his work with Anna O. – a woman suffering with symptoms of paralysis, anaesthesias, and disturbances of vision and speech. The discussions of Anna O. between Freud and Breuer were documented in their Studies in Hysteria and became a formative basis of Freudian theory and psychoanalytic practice.
Nervous system	The body's electrochemical communication circuitry, made up of billions of neurons is a nervous system.
Lesion	A lesion is a non-specific term referring to abnormal tissue in the body. It can be caused by any disease process including trauma (physical, chemical, electrical), infection, neoplasm, metabolic and autoimmune.
Clinical method	Studying psychological problems and therapies in clinical settings is referred to as the clinical method. It usually involves case histories, pathology, or non-experimentally controlled environments.
Nerve	A nerve is an enclosed, cable-like bundle of nerve fibers or axons, which includes the glia that ensheath the axons in myelin. Neurons are sometimes called nerve cells, though this term is technically imprecise since many neurons do not form nerves.
Preconscious	In psychodynamic theory, material that is not in awareness but that can be brought into awareness by focusing one's attention is referred to as preconscious.
Mental processes	The thoughts, feelings, and motives that each of us experiences privately but that cannot be observed directly are called mental processes.
Amnesia	Amnesia is a condition in which memory is disturbed. The causes of amnesia are organic or functional. Organic causes include damage to the brain, through trauma or disease, or use of certain (generally sedative) drugs.
Unconscious mind	The unconscious mind refers to information processing and brain functioning of which a person is unaware. In Freudian theory, it is the repository of unacceptable thoughts and feelings.
Clinician	A health professional authorized to provide services to people suffering from one or more pathologies is a clinician.
Conversion hysteria	Conversion hysteria is an obsolete term for conversion disorder derived from the Freudian notion that physical symptoms represented a conversion of unconscious conflicts into a more acceptable form.
Mutism	Mutism refers to refusal or inability to talk.
Tics	Tics are a repeated, impulsive action, almost reflexive in nature, which the person feels powerless to control or avoid.
Hilgard	Hilgard made headlines as a pioneer in the scientific study of hypnosis. He and his wife, Josephine, established the Laboratory of Hypnosis Research at Stanford.
Personality disorder	A mental disorder characterized by a set of inflexible, maladaptive personality traits that keep a person from functioning properly in society is referred to as a personality disorder.

Go to **Cram101.com** for the Practice Tests for this Chapter.

Control subjects	Control subjects are participants in an experiment who do not receive the treatment effect but for whom all other conditions are held comparable to those of experimental subjects.
Mental disorder	Mental disorder refers to a disturbance in a person's emotions, drives, thought processes, or behavior that involves serious and relatively prolonged distress and/or impairment in ability to function, is not simply a normal response to some event or set of events in the person's environment.
Psychosis	Psychosis is a generic term for mental states in which the components of rational thought and perception are severely impaired. Persons experiencing a psychosis may experience hallucinations, hold paranoid or delusional beliefs, demonstrate personality changes and exhibit disorganized thinking. This is usually accompanied by features such as a lack of insight into the unusual or bizarre nature of their behavior, difficulties with social interaction and impairments in carrying out the activities of daily living.
Hallucination	A hallucination is a sensory perception experienced in the absence of an external stimulus, as distinct from an illusion, which is a misperception of an external stimulus. They may occur in any sensory modality - visual, auditory, olfactory, gustatory, tactile, or mixed.
Psychotic behavior	A psychotic behavior is a severe psychological disorder characterized by hallucinations and loss of contact with reality.
Manifest content	In psychodynamic theory, the reported content of dreams is referred to as manifest content.
Latent content	In psychodynamic theory, the symbolized or underlying content of dreams is called latent content.
Dream symbols	Images in dreams whose personal or emotional meanings differ from their literal meanings are called dream symbols.
Coding	In senation, coding is the process by which information about the quality and quantity of a stimulus is preserved in the pattern of action potentials sent through sensory neurons to the central nervous system.
Trauma	Trauma refers to a severe physical injury or wound to the body caused by an external force, or a psychological shock having a lasting effect on mental life.
Mind-body problem	There are three basic views of the mind-body problem: mental and physical events are totally different, and cannot be reduced to each other (dualism); mental events are to be reduced to physical events (materialism); and physical events are to be reduced to mental events (phenomenalism).
Neurotransmitter	A neurotransmitter is a chemical that is used to relay, amplify and modulate electrical signals between a neurons and another cell.
Personality test	A personality test aims to describe aspects of a person's character that remain stable across situations.
Attachment	Attachment is the tendency to seek closeness to another person and feel secure when that person is present.
Emotion	An emotion is a mental states that arise spontaneously, rather than through conscious effort. They are often accompanied by physiological changes.
Guilt	Guilt describes many concepts related to a negative emotion or condition caused by actions which are believed to be, morally wrong. According to Freud, the avoidance of guilt is the basis for moral behavior.
Forebrain	The forebrain is the highest level of the brain. Key structures in the forebrain are the limbic system, thalamus, basal ganglia, hypothalamus, and cerebral cortex.

Go to **Cram101.com** for the Practice Tests for this Chapter.

Pons	The pons is a knob on the brain stem. It is part of the autonomic nervous system, and relays sensory information between the cerebellum and cerebrum. Some theories posit that it has a role in dreaming.
Displacement	An unconscious defense mechanism in which the individual directs aggressive or sexual feelings away from the primary object to someone or something safe is referred to as displacement. Displacement in linguistics is simply the ability to talk about things not present.
Psychopathology	Psychopathology refers to the field concerned with the nature and development of mental disorders.
Parapraxes	Parapraxes or Freudian slip is an error in human action, speech or memory that is believed to be caused by the unconscious mind. The error often appears to the observer as being casual, bizarre or nonsensical.
Freudian slip	The Freudian slip is named after Sigmund Freud, who described the phenomenon he called faulty action in his 1901 book The Psychopathology of Everyday Life. The Freudian slip is an error in human action, speech or memory that is believed to be caused by the unconscious mind.
Tact	The word tact, another of Skinner's intentionally "nonsense" words, comes from the notion of the child's making "conTACT" with the nonverbal environment. The tact is verbal behavior that is under the control of the nonverbal environment and includes nouns, actions, adjectives, pronouns, relations, and others.
Feedback	Feedback refers to information returned to a person about the effects a response has had.
Attitude	An enduring mental representation of a person, place, or thing that evokes an emotional response and related behavior is called attitude.
Prejudice	Prejudice in general, implies coming to a judgment on the subject before learning where the preponderance of the evidence actually lies, or formation of a judgement without direct experience.
Thematic Apperception Test	The Thematic Apperception Test uses a standard series of provocative yet ambiguous pictures about which the subject must tell a story. Each story is carefully analyzed to uncover underlying needs, attitudes, and patterns of reaction.
Apperception	A newly experienced sensation is related to past experiences to form an understood situation. For Wundt, consciousness is composed of two "stages:" There is a large capacity working memory called the Blickfeld and the narrower consciousness called Apperception, or selective attention.
Stimulus	A change in an environmental condition that elicits a response is a stimulus.
Social motives	Social motives refer to drives acquired through experience and interaction with others.
Motives	Needs or desires that energize and direct behavior toward a goal are motives.
Hypothesis	A specific statement about behavior or mental processes that is testable through research is a hypothesis.
Superego	Frued's third psychic structure, which functions as a moral guardian and sets forth high standards for behavior is the superego.
Metaphor	A metaphor is a rhetorical trope where a comparison is made between two seemingly unrelated subjects
Pleasure principle	The pleasure principle is the tendency to seek pleasure and avoid pain. In Freud's theory, this principle rules the Id, but is at least partly repressed by the reality principle.
Socialization	Social rules and social relations are created, communicated, and changed in verbal and

	nonverbal ways creating social complexity useful in identifying outsiders and intelligent breeding partners. The process of learning these skills is called socialization.
Death instinct	The death instinct was defined by Sigmund Freud, in Beyond the Pleasure Principle(1920). It speculated on the existence of a fundamental death wish or death instinct, referring to an individual's own need to die.
Eros	In Freudian psychology, Eros is the life instinct innate in all humans. It is the desire to create life and favours productivity and construction. Eros battles against the destructive death instinct of Thanatos.
Innate	Innate behavior is not learned or influenced by the environment, rather, it is present or predisposed at birth.
Biological needs	Beyond physiological needs for survival, the next level are motivations that have an obvious biological basis but are not required for the immediate survival of the organism. These biological needs include the powerful motivations for sex, parenting and aggression.
Homeostasis	Homeostasis is the property of an open system, especially living organisms, to regulate its internal environment so as to maintain a stable condition, by means of multiple dynamic equilibrium adjustments controlled by interrelated regulation mechanisms.
Cathexis	Tolman's cathexis is the acquisition of a connection between a given goal object and the corresponding drive for it.
Plasticity	The capacity for modification and change is referred to as plasticity.
Primary process	The primary process in psychoanalytic theory, is one of the id's means of reducing tension by imagining what it desires.
Wish fulfillment	A primitive method used by the id to attempt to gratify basic instincts is referred to as wish fulfillment.
Punishment	Punishment is the addtion of a stimulus that reduces the frequency of a response, or the removal of a stimulus that results in a reduction of the response.
Intrapsychic conflict	In psychoanalysis, the struggles among the id, ego, and superego are an intrapsychic conflict.
Executive function	The processes involved in regulating attention and in determining what to do with information just gathered or retrieved from long-term memory, is referred to as the executive function.
Anagram	An anagram is a type of word play, the result of rearranging the letters of a word or phrase to produce other words, using all the original letters exactly once.
Suppression	Suppression is the defense mechanism where a memory is deliberately forgotten.
Neurotic anxiety	Neurotic anxiety refers to, in psychoanalytic theory, a fear of the consequences of expressing previously punished and repressed id impulses; more generally, unrealistic fear.
Moral anxiety	In psychoanalytic theory, the ego's fear of punishment for failure to adhere to the superego's standards of proper conduct is referred to as moral anxiety.
Reaction formation	In Freud's psychoanalytic theory, reaction formation is a defense mechanism in which anxiety-producing or unacceptable emotions are replaced by their direct opposites.
Rationalization	Rationalization is the process of constructing a logical justification for a decision that was originally arrived at through a different mental process. It is one of Freud's defense mechanisms.
Longitudinal study	Longitudinal study is a type of developmental study in which the same group of participants is followed and measured for an extended period of time, often years.

Go to **Cram101.com** for the Practice Tests for this Chapter.

Maladaptive	In psychology, a behavior or trait is adaptive when it helps an individual adjust and function well within their social environment. A maladaptive behavior or trait is counterproductive to the individual.
Projection	Attributing one's own undesirable thoughts, impulses, traits, or behaviors to others is referred to as projection.
Homosexual	Homosexual refers to a sexual orientation characterized by aesthetic attraction, romantic love, and sexual desire exclusively for members of the same sex or gender identity.
Penis	The penis is the external male copulatory organ and the external male organ of urination. In humans, the penis is homologous to the female clitoris, as it develops from the same embryonic structure. It is capable of erection for use in copulation.
Personality trait	According to the Diagnostic and Statistical Manual of the American Psychiatric Association, a personality trait is a "prominent aspect of personality that is exhibited in a wide range of important social and personal contexts. ...".
Super-ego	The Super-ego stands in opposition to the desires of the Id. The Super-ego is based upon the internalization of the world view, norms and mores a child absorbs from parents and the surrounding environment at a young age. As the conscience, it includes our sense of right and wrong, maintaining taboos specific to a child's internalization of parental culture.
Creativity	Creativity is the ability to think about something in novel and unusual ways and come up with unique solutions to problems. It involves divergent thinking, having many solutions or views to a problem.
Regression	Return to a form of behavior characteristic of an earlier stage of development is called regression.
Reliability	Reliability means the extent to which a test produces a consistent , reproducible score .
Experimental manipulation	The change that an experimenter deliberately produces in a situation under study is called the experimental manipulation.
Self-report inventories	Personality tests that ask individuals to answer a series of questions about their own characteristic behaviors are called self-report inventories.
Self-report method	The self-report method is an experimental design in which the people being studied are asked to rate or describe their own behaviors or mental states.
Questionnaire	A self-report method of data collection or clinical assessment method in which the individual being studied checks off items on a printed list, answers multiple-choice questions, or writes out answers to essay questions aimed at producing a selfdescription is called questionnaire.
Self-image	A person's self-image is the mental picture, generally of a kind that is quite resistant to change, that depicts not only details that are potentially available to objective investigation by others, but also items that have been learned by that person about himself or herself.
Erogenous zone	An erogenous zone is an area of the human body that has heightened sensitivity and stimulation normally results in sexual response.
Infancy	The developmental period that extends from birth to 18 or 24 months is called infancy.
Anal stage	The anal stage in psychology is the term used by Sigmund Freud to describe the development during the second year of life, in which a child's pleasure and conflict centers are in the anal area.
Toddler	A toddler is a child between the ages of one and three years old. During this period, the

28

	child learns a great deal about social roles and develops motor skills; to toddle is to walk unsteadily.
Phallic stage	The phallic stage is the 3rd of Freud's psychosexual stages, when awareness of and manipulation of the genitals is supposed to be a primary source of pleasure. In this stage the child deals with the Oedipus complex, if male, or the Electra Complex, if female.
Masturbation	Masturbation is the manual excitation of the sexual organs, most often to the point of orgasm. It can refer to excitation either by oneself or by another, but commonly refers to such activities performed alone.
Incest	Incest refers to sexual relations between close relatives, most often between daughter and father or between brother and sister.
Dissociation	Dissociation is a psychological state or condition in which certain thoughts, emotions, sensations, or memories are separated from the rest.
Psychosexual stages	In Freudian theory each child passes through five psychosexual stages. During each stage, the id focuses on a distinct erogenous zone on the body. Suffering from trauma during any of the first three stages may result in fixation in that stage. Freud related the resolutions of the stages with adult personalities and personality disorders.
Oral stage	The oral stage in psychology is the term used by Sigmund Freud to describe the development during the first eighteen months of life, in which an infant's pleasure centers are in the mouth. This is the first of Freud's psychosexual stages.
Sadism	Sadism is the sexual pleasure or gratification in the infliction of pain and suffering upon another person. It is considered to be a paraphilia. The word is derived from the name of the Marquis de Sade, a prolific French writer of sadistic novels.
Personality type	A persistent style of complex behaviors defined by a group of related traits is referred to as a personality type. Myer Friedman and his co-workers first defined personality types in the 1950s. Friedman classified people into 2 categories, Type A and Type B.
Oral fixation	An oral fixation is a fixation in the oral stage of development and manifested by an obsession with stimulating the mouth, first described by Sigmund Freud.
Anal retentive	A person characterized as anal retentive is perceived to be worrying too much about "nit-picking" little details of form, style and etiquette or otherwise being overly uptight or distressed over ordinarily minor problems.
Castration	Castration is any action, surgical, chemical or otherwise, by which a biological male loses use of the testes. This causes sterilization, i.e. prevents him from reproducing; it also greatly reduces the production of certain hormones, such as testosterone.
Castration anxiety	Castration anxiety is a fear posited by Sigmund Freud in his writings on the Oedipus complex at the genital stage of sexual development. It asserts that boys seeing a girl's genitalia will falsely assume that the girl must have had her penis removed, probably as punishment for some misbehavior, and will be anxious lest the same happen to him.
Oedipus complex	The Oedipus complex is a concept developed by Sigmund Freud to explain the maturation of the infant boy through identification with the father and desire for the mother.
Syphilis	Syphilis is a sexually transmitted disease that is caused by a spirochaete bacterium, Treponema pallidum. If not treated, syphilis can cause serious effects such as damage to the nervous system, heart, or brain. Untreated syphilis can be ultimately fatal.
Internalization	The developmental change from behavior that is externally controlled to behavior that is controlled by internal standards and principles is referred to as internalization.
Clitoris	Clitoris refers to an external female sex organ that is highly sensitive to sexual

stimulation.

Masculinity	Masculinity is a culturally determined value reflecting the set of characteristics of maleness.
Femininity	Femininity is the set of characteristics defined by a culture for idealized females.
Neurosis	Neurosis, any mental disorder that, although may cause distress, does not interfere with rational thought or the persons' ability to function.
Masochism	The counterpart of sadism is masochism, the sexual pleasure or gratification of having pain or suffering inflicted upon the self, often consisting of sexual fantasies or urges for being beaten, humiliated, bound, tortured, or otherwise made to suffer, either as an enhancement to or a substitute for sexual pleasure.
Bisexuality	Bisexuality is a sexual orientation characterized by aesthetic attraction, romantic love and sexual desire for both males and females.
Sexual orientation	Sexual orientation refers to the sex or gender of people who are the focus of a person's amorous or erotic desires, fantasies, and spontaneous feelings, the gender(s) toward which one is primarily "oriented".
Oedipus conflict	For Freud, a child's sexual interest in his or her opposite-sex parent, typically resolved through identification with the same-sex parent, is an Oedipus conflict.
Prenatal	Prenatal period refers to the time from conception to birth.
Hormone	A hormone is a chemical messenger from one cell (or group of cells) to another. The best known are those produced by endocrine glands, but they are produced by nearly every organ system. The function of hormones is to serve as a signal to the target cells; the action of the hormone is determined by the pattern of secretion and the signal transduction of the receiving tissue.
Schizophrenia	Schizophrenia is characterized by persistent defects in the perception or expression of reality. A person suffering from untreated schizophrenia typically demonstrates grossly disorganized thinking, and may also experience delusions or auditory hallucinations
Latency stage	Sigmund Freud suggested that the latency stage, age 6-10, this was a time of sexual latency, when the healthy child ceased all sexual interest and was vulnerable to trauma if he or she experienced sexuality.
Paranoia	In popular culture, the term paranoia is usually used to describe excessive concern about one's own well-being, sometimes suggesting a person holds persecutory beliefs concerning a threat to themselves or their property and is often linked to a belief in conspiracy theories.
Latency	In child development, latency refers to a phase of psychosexual development characterized by repression of sexual impulses. In learning theory, latency is the delay between stimulus (S) and response (R), which according to Hull depends on the strength of the association.
Genital stage	The genital stage in psychology is the term used by Sigmund Freud to describe the final stage of human psychosexual development. It is characterized by the expression of libido through intercourse with an adult of the other gender.
Puberty	Puberty refers to the process of physical changes by which a child's body becomes an adult body capable of reproduction.
Sexual dysfunction	Sexual dysfunction or sexual malfunction is difficulty during any stage of the sexual act (which includes desire, arousal, orgasm, and resolution) that prevents the individual or couple from enjoying sexual activity.

Go to **Cram101.com** for the Practice Tests for this Chapter.

Free association	In psychoanalysis, the uncensored uttering of all thoughts that come to mind is called free association.
Compulsion	An apparently irresistible urge to repeat an act or engage in ritualistic behavior such as hand washing is referred to as a compulsion.
Psychological test	Psychological test refers to a standardized measure of a sample of a person's behavior.
Catharsis	Catharsis has been adopted by modern psychotherapy as the act of giving expression to deep emotions often associated with events in the individuals past which have never before been adequately expressed.
Insight	Insight refers to a sudden awareness of the relationships among various elements that had previously appeared to be independent of one another.
Transference	Transference is a phenomenon in psychology characterized by unconscious redirection of feelings from one person to another.
Countertransference	Feelings that the psychoanalyst unconsciously directs to the analysis, stemming from his or her own emotional vulnerabilities and unresolved conflicts are countertransference effects.
Medical model	The medical model views abnormal behavior as a disease.
Mental illness	Mental illness is the term formerly used to mean psychological disorder but less preferred because it implies that the causes of the disorder can be found in a medical disease process.
Wisdom	Wisdom is the ability to make correct judgments and decisions. It is an intangible quality gained through experience. Whether or not something is wise is determined in a pragmatic sense by its popularity, how long it has been around, and its ability to predict against future events.
Szasz	Szasz is a critic of the moral and scientific foundations of psychiatry. He argues that the belief that mental illness is a real illness has hurt many more people than it has helped. He is well known for his books The Myth of Mental Illness and The Manufacture of Madness: A Comparative Study of the Inquisition and the Mental Health Movement.
Premise	A premise is a statement presumed true within the context of a discourse, especially of a logical argument.
Psychosomatic	A psychosomatic illness is one with physical manifestations and perhaps a supposed psychological cause. It is often diagnosed when any known or identifiable physical cause was excluded by medical examination.
Phobia	A persistent, irrational fear of an object, situation, or activity that the person feels compelled to avoid is referred to as a phobia.
Fisher	Fisher was a eugenicist, evolutionary biologist, geneticist and statistician. He has been described as "The greatest of Darwin's successors", and a genius who almost single-handedly created the foundations for modern statistical science inventing the techniques of maximum likelihood and analysis of variance.
Psychodynamic therapy	Psychodynamic therapy uses a range of different techniques, applied to the client considering his or her needs. Most approaches are centered around the idea of a maladapted function developed early in life which are at least in part unconscious.
Wolpe	Wolpe is best known for applying classical conditioning principles to the treatment of phobias, called systematic desensitization. Any "neutral" stimulus, simple or complex that happens to make an impact on an individual at about the time that a fear reaction is evoked acquires the ability to evoke fear subsequently. An acquired CS-CR relationship should be extinguishable.

Go to **Cram101.com** for the Practice Tests for this Chapter.

Eating disorders	Psychological disorders characterized by distortion of the body image and gross disturbances in eating patterns are called eating disorders.
Loftus	Loftus works on human memory and how it can be changed by facts, ideas, suggestions and other forms of post-event information. One of her famous studies include the "car accident" study, which was an example of the misinformation effect.
Repressed memory	A repressed memory, according to some theories of psychology, is a memory (often traumatic) of an event or environment which is stored by the unconscious mind but outside the awareness of the conscious mind.
Child abuse	Child abuse is the physical or psychological maltreatment of a child.
Polygraph	A polygraph is a device which measures and records several physiological variables such as blood pressure, heart rate, respiration and skin conductivity while a series of questions is being asked, in an attempt to detect lies.
Prospective study	Prospective study is a long-term study of a group of people, beginning before the onset of a common disorder. It allows investigators to see how the disorder develops.
Laboratory study	Any research study in which the subjects are brought to a specially designated area that has been set up to facilitate the researcher's ability to control the environment or collect data is referred to as a laboratory study.
Survey	A method of scientific investigation in which a large sample of people answer questions about their attitudes or behavior is referred to as a survey.
Borderline personality disorder	Borderline personality disorder is characterized by extreme 'black and white' thinking, mood swings, emotional reasoning, disrupted relationships and difficulty in functioning in a way society accepts as normal.
Stress disorder	A significant emotional disturbance caused by stresses outside the range of normal human experience is referred to as stress disorder.
Subliminal message	A subliminal message is a signal or message designed to pass below the normal limits of perception. For example it might be inaudible to the conscious mind or might be an image transmitted briefly and unperceived consciously and yet perceived unconsciously.
Pathology	Pathology is the study of the processes underlying disease and other forms of illness, harmful abnormality, or dysfunction.
Cognition	The intellectual processes through which information is obtained, transformed, stored, retrieved, and otherwise used is cognition.
Subliminal presentation	A method of presenting stimuli so faintly or rapidly that people do not have any conscious awareness of having been exposed to them is a subliminal presentation.
Neural network	A clusters of neurons that is interconnected to process information is referred to as a neural network.
Individual differences	Individual differences psychology studies the ways in which individual people differ in their behavior. This is distinguished from other aspects of psychology in that although psychology is ostensibly a study of individuals, modern psychologists invariably study groups.
Hippocampus	The hippocampus is a part of the brain located inside the temporal lobe. It forms a part of the limbic system and plays a part in memory and navigation.
Neuroscience	A field that combines the work of psychologists, biologists, biochemists, medical researchers, and others in the study of the structure and function of the nervous system is neuroscience.
Right hemisphere	The brain is divided into left and right cerebral hemispheres. The right hemisphere of the

Go to Cram101.com for the Practice Tests for this Chapter.

cortex controls the left side of the body.

Brain imaging	Brain imaging is a fairly recent discipline within medicine and neuroscience. Brain imaging falls into two broad categories -- structural imaging and functional imaging.
Delusion	A false belief, not generally shared by others, and that cannot be changed despite strong evidence to the contrary is a delusion.
Secondary process	Secondary process is the mental activity and thinking characteristic of the ego, influenced by the demands of the environment. Characterized by organization, systematization, intellectualization, and similar processes leading to logical thought and action in adult life.
Reality principle	The reality principle tells us to subordinate pleasure to what needs to be done. Subordinating the pleasure principle to the reality principle is done through a psychological process Freud calls sublimation, where you take desires that can't be fulfilled, or shouldn't be fulfilled, and turn their energy into something useful and productive.
Ego ideal	The component of the superego that involves ideal standards approved by parents is called ego ideal. The ego ideal rewards the child by conveying a sense of pride and personal value when the child acts according to ideal standards.
Empirical evidence	Facts or information based on direct observation or experience are referred to as empirical evidence.

Go to **Cram101.com** for the Practice Tests for this Chapter.

Analytical psychology	Analytical psychology is based upon the movement started by Carl Jung and his followers as distinct from Freudian psychoanalysis. Its aim is the personal experience of the deep forces and motivations underlying human behavior.
Archetype	The archetype is a concept of psychologist Carl Jung. They are innate prototypes for ideas, which may subsequently become involved in the interpretation of observed phenomena. A group of memories and interpretations closely associated with an archetype is called a complex.
Jung	Jung was in some aspects a response to Sigmund Freud's psychoanalysis. He proposed and developed the concepts of the extroverted and introverted personality, archetypes, and the collective unconscious. His work has been influential in psychiatry and in the study of religion, literature, and related fields.
Psyche	Psyche is the soul, spirit, or mind as distinguished from the body. In psychoanalytic theory, it is the totality of the id, ego, and superego, including both conscious and unconscious components.
Introvert	Introvert refers to a person whose attention is focused inward; a shy, reserved, timid person.
Motivation	In psychology, motivation is the driving force (desire) behind all actions of an organism.
Consciousness	The awareness of the sensations, thoughts, and feelings being experienced at a given moment is called consciousness.
Script	A schema, or behavioral sequence, for an event is called a script. It is a form of schematic organization, with real-world events organized in terms of temporal and causal relations between component acts.
Psychoanalytic	Freud's theory that unconscious forces act as determinants of personality is called psychoanalytic theory. The theory is a developmental theory characterized by critical stages of development.
Personality type	A persistent style of complex behaviors defined by a group of related traits is referred to as a personality type. Myer Friedman and his co-workers first defined personality types in the 1950s. Friedman classified people into 2 categories, Type A and Type B.
Psychotherapy	Psychotherapy is a set of techniques based on psychological principles intended to improve mental health, emotional or behavioral issues.
Personality	Personality refers to the pattern of enduring characteristics that differentiates a person, the patterns of behaviors that make each individual unique.
Intuition	Quick, impulsive thought that does not make use of formal logic or clear reasoning is referred to as intuition.
Perception	Perception is the process of acquiring, interpreting, selecting, and organizing sensory information.
Collective unconscious	Collective unconscious is a term of analytical psychology, originally coined by Carl Jung. It refers to that part of a person's unconscious which is common to all human beings. It contains archetypes, which are forms or symbols that are manifested by all people in all cultures.
Scientific method	Psychologists gather data in order to describe, understand, predict, and control behavior. Scientific method refers to an approach that can be used to discover accurate information. It includes these steps: understand the problem, collect data, draw conclusions, and revise research conclusions.
Empirical	Empirical means the use of working hypotheses which are capable of being disproved using observation or experiment.

Goethe	Goethe argued that laws could not be created by pure rationalism, since geography and history shaped habits and patterns. This stood in sharp contrast to the prevailing Enlightenment view that reason was sufficient to create well-ordered societies and good laws.
Dissociation	Dissociation is a psychological state or condition in which certain thoughts, emotions, sensations, or memories are separated from the rest.
Pathology	Pathology is the study of the processes underlying disease and other forms of illness, harmful abnormality, or dysfunction.
Ego	In Freud's view the Ego serves to balance our primitive needs and our moral beliefs and taboos. Relying on experience, a healthy Ego provides the ability to adapt to reality and interact with the outside world.
Superego	Frued's third psychic structure, which functions as a moral guardian and sets forth high standards for behavior is the superego.
Libido	Sigmund Freud suggested that libido is the instinctual energy or force that can come into conflict with the conventions of civilized behavior. Jung, condidered the libido as the free creative, or psychic, energy an individual has to put toward personal development, or individuation.
Learning	Learning is a relatively permanent change in behavior that results from experience. Thus, to attribute a behavioral change to learning, the change must be relatively permanent and must result from experience.
Compensation	In personaility, compensation, according to Adler, is an effort to overcome imagined or real inferiorities by developing one's abilities.
Homeostasis	Homeostasis is the property of an open system, especially living organisms, to regulate its internal environment so as to maintain a stable condition, by means of multiple dynamic equilibrium adjustments controlled by interrelated regulation mechanisms.
Metaphor	A metaphor is a rhetorical trope where a comparison is made between two seemingly unrelated subjects
Anxiety	Anxiety is a complex combination of the feeling of fear, apprehension and worry often accompanied by physical sensations such as palpitations, chest pain and/or shortness of breath.
Attention	Attention is the cognitive process of selectively concentrating on one thing while ignoring other things. Psychologists have labeled three types of attention: sustained attention, selective attention, and divided attention.
Neurosis	Neurosis, any mental disorder that, although may cause distress, does not interfere with rational thought or the persons' ability to function.
Projection	Attributing one's own undesirable thoughts, impulses, traits, or behaviors to others is referred to as projection.
Personal identity	The portion of the self-concept that pertains to the self as a distinct, separate individual is called personal identity.
Persona	In Jungian archetypal psychology, the Persona is the mask or appearance one presents to the world. It may appear in dreams under various guises.
Society	The social sciences use the term society to mean a group of people that form a semi-closed (or semi-open) social system, in which most interactions are with other individuals belonging to the group.
Self-image	A person's self-image is the mental picture, generally of a kind that is quite resistant to

change, that depicts not only details that are potentially available to objective investigation by others, but also items that have been learned by that person about himself or herself.

Social role	Social role refers to expected behavior patterns associated with particular social positions.
Anima	Anima, according to Carl Jung, is the feminine side of a man's personal unconscious. It can be identified as all the unconscious feminine psychological qualities that a man possesses.
Self-concept	Self-concept refers to domain-specific evaluations of the self where a domain may be academics, athletics, etc.
Psychiatrist	A psychiatrist is a physician who specializes in the diagnosis and treatment of psychological disorders.
Suicide	Suicide behavior is rare in childhood but escalates in adolescence. The suicide rate increases in a linear fashion from adolescence through late adulthood.
Creativity	Creativity is the ability to think about something in novel and unusual ways and come up with unique solutions to problems. It involves divergent thinking, having many solutions or views to a problem.
Prejudice	Prejudice in general, implies coming to a judgment on the subject before learning where the preponderance of the evidence actually lies, or formation of a judgement without direct experience.
Eros	In Freudian psychology, Eros is the life instinct innate in all humans. It is the desire to create life and favours productivity and construction. Eros battles against the destructive death instinct of Thanatos.
Self-report inventories	Personality tests that ask individuals to answer a series of questions about their own characteristic behaviors are called self-report inventories.
Individual differences	Individual differences psychology studies the ways in which individual people differ in their behavior. This is distinguished from other aspects of psychology in that although psychology is ostensibly a study of individuals, modern psychologists invariably study groups.
Masculinity	Masculinity is a culturally determined value reflecting the set of characteristics of maleness.
Femininity	Femininity is the set of characteristics defined by a culture for idealized females.
Sexism	Sexism is commonly considered to be discrimination against people based on their sex rather than their individual merits, but can also refer to any and all differentiations based on
Androgyny	Androgyny refers to two concepts. The first is the mixing of masculine and feminine characteristics. Secondly it describes something that is neither masculine nor feminine.
Personal unconscious	The personal unconscious in Jung's theory is the layer of the unconscious containing all of the thoughts and experiences that are accessible to the conscious, as well as the repressed memories and impulses.
Androgynous	Having both typical feminine and masculine characteristics is androgynous.
Brain	The brain controls and coordinates most movement, behavior and homeostatic body functions such as heartbeat, blood pressure, fluid balance and body temperature. Functions of the brain are responsible for cognition, emotion, memory, motor learning and other sorts of learning. The brain is primarily made up of two types of cells: glia and neurons.
Species	Species refers to a reproductively isolated breeding population.
Physiological	Physiological psychology refers to the study of the physiological mechanisms, in the brain

psychology	and elsewhere, that mediate behavior and psychological experiences.
Sensation	Sensation is the first stage in the chain of biochemical and neurologic events that begins with the impinging of a stimulus upon the receptor cells of a sensory organ, which then leads to perception, the mental state that is reflected in statements like "I see a uniformly blue wall."
Neuron	The neuron is the primary cell of the nervous system. They are found in the brain, the spinal cord, in the nerves and ganglia of the peripheral nervous system. It is a specialized cell that conducts impulses through the nervous system and contains three major parts: cell body, dendrites, and an axon. It can have many dendrites but only one axon.
Psychosomatic	A psychosomatic illness is one with physical manifestations and perhaps a supposed psychological cause. It is often diagnosed when any known or identifiable physical cause was excluded by medical examination.
Neuroscience	A field that combines the work of psychologists, biologists, biochemists, medical researchers, and others in the study of the structure and function of the nervous system is neuroscience.
Stimulus	A change in an environmental condition that elicits a response is a stimulus.
Amygdala	Located in the brain's medial temporal lobe, the almond-shaped amygdala is believed to play a key role in the emotions. It forms part of the limbic system and is linked to both fear responses and pleasure. Its size is positively correlated with aggressive behavior across species.
Lesion	A lesion is a non-specific term referring to abnormal tissue in the body. It can be caused by any disease process including trauma (physical, chemical, electrical), infection, neoplasm, metabolic and autoimmune.
Innate	Innate behavior is not learned or influenced by the environment, rather, it is present or predisposed at birth.
Genetics	Genetics is the science of genes, heredity, and the variation of organisms.
Psychoanalyst	A psychoanalyst is a specially trained therapist who attempts to treat the individual by uncovering and revealing to the individual otherwise subconscious factors that are contributing to some undesirable behavor.
Ethnic group	An ethnic group is a culture or subculture whose members are readily distinguishable by outsiders based on traits originating from a common racial, national, linguistic, or religious source. Members of an ethnic group are often presumed to be culturally or biologically similar, although this is not in fact necessarily the case.
Predisposition	Predisposition refers to an inclination or diathesis to respond in a certain way, either inborn or acquired. In abnormal psychology, it is a factor that lowers the ability to withstand stress and inclines the individual toward pathology.
Trait	An enduring personality characteristic that tends to lead to certain behaviors is called a trait. The term trait also means a genetically inherited feature of an organism.
Individuality	According to Cooper, individuality consists of two dimensions: self-assertion and separateness.
Meditation	Meditation usually refers to a state in which the body is consciously relaxed and the mind is allowed to become calm and focused.
Psychosis	Psychosis is a generic term for mental states in which the components of rational thought and perception are severely impaired. Persons experiencing a psychosis may experience hallucinations, hold paranoid or delusional beliefs, demonstrate personality changes and

exhibit disorganized thinking. This is usually accompanied by features such as a lack of insight into the unusual or bizarre nature of their behavior, difficulties with social interaction and impairments in carrying out the activities of daily living.

Heredity	Heredity is the transfer of characteristics from parent to offspring through their genes.
Validity	The extent to which a test measures what it is intended to measure is called validity.
Emotion	An emotion is a mental states that arise spontaneously, rather than through conscious effort. They are often accompanied by physiological changes.
Insight	Insight refers to a sudden awareness of the relationships among various elements that had previously appeared to be independent of one another.
Evolution	Commonly used to refer to gradual change, evolution is the change in the frequency of alleles within a population from one generation to the next. This change may be caused by different mechanisms, including natural selection, genetic drift, or changes in population (gene flow).
Wisdom	Wisdom is the ability to make correct judgments and decisions. It is an intangible quality gained through experience. Whether or not something is wise is determined in a pragmatic sense by its popularity, how long it has been around, and its ability to predict against future events.
Attitude	An enduring mental representation of a person, place, or thing that evokes an emotional response and related behavior is called attitude.
Psychoanalysis	Psychoanalysis refers to the school of psychology that emphasizes the importance of unconscious motives and conflicts as determinants of human behavior. It was Freud's method of exploring human personality.
Construct	A generalized concept, such as anxiety or gravity, is a construct.
Rorschach	The Rorschach inkblot test is a method of psychological evaluation. It is a projective test associated with the Freudian school of thought. Psychologists use this test to try to probe the unconscious minds of their patients.
Heuristic	A heuristic is a simple, efficient rule of thumb proposed to explain how people make decisions, come to judgments and solve problems, typically when facing complex problems or incomplete information. These rules work well under most circumstances, but in certain cases lead to systematic cognitive biases.
Extrasensory perception	Extrasensory perception refers to gaining awareness of or information about objects, events, or another's thoughts through some means other than the known sensory channels.
Telepathy	Telepathy is the claimed innate ability of humans and other creatures to communicate information from one mind to another, without the use of extra tools such as speech or body language.
Sympathetic	The sympathetic nervous system activates what is often termed the "fight or flight response". It is an automatic regulation system, that is, one that operates without the intervention of conscious thought.
Synchronicity	Jung's concept of synchronicity describes the alignment of universal forces with the life experiences of an individual. Jung believed that many experiences perceived as coincidences were not merely due to chance, but instead reflected the creation of an event or circumstance by the alignment of such forces.
Introversion	A personality trait characterized by intense imagination and a tendency to inhibit impulses is called introversion.
Extraversion	Extraversion, one of the big-five personailty traits, is marked by pronounced engagement with

Go to **Cram101.com** for the Practice Tests for this Chapter.

	the external world. They are people who enjoy being with people, are full of energy, and often experience positive emotions.
Subjective experience	Subjective experience refers to reality as it is perceived and interpreted, not as it exists objectively.
Spock	Spock was an American pediatrician whose book Baby and Child Care, published in 1946, is one of the biggest best-sellers of all time. Its revolutionary message to mothers was that "you know more than you think you do." Spock was the first pediatrician to study psychoanalysis to try to understand children's needs and family dynamics.
Repression	A defense mechanism, repression involves moving thoughts unacceptable to the ego into the unconscious, where they cannot be easily accessed.
Emotional intelligence	The expression emotional intelligence indicates a kind of intelligence or skill that involves the ability to perceive, assess and positively influence one's own and other people's emotions.
Mayer	Mayer developed the concept of emotional intelligence with Peter Salovey. He is one of the authors of the Mayer-Salovey-Caruso Emotional Intelligence Test, and has developed a new, integrated framework for personality psychology, known as the Systems Framework for Pesronality Psychology.
Senses	The senses are systems that consist of a sensory cell type that respond to a specific kind of physical energy, and that correspond to a defined region within the brain where the signals are received and interpreted.
Inference	Inference is the act or process of drawing a conclusion based solely on what one already knows.
Cognition	The intellectual processes through which information is obtained, transformed, stored, retrieved, and otherwise used is cognition.
Myers-Briggs	The Myers-Briggs Type Indicator is a psychological test designed to assist a person in identifying their personality preferences. It follows from the theories of Carl Jung. The types tested for, known as dichotomies, are extraversion, introversion, sensing, intuition, thinking, feeling, judging and perceiving.
Population	Population refers to all members of a well-defined group of organisms, events, or things.
Brainstorming	Brainstorming is an organized approach for producing ideas by letting the mind think without interruption. The term was coined by Alex Osborn.
Correlation	A statistical technique for determining the degree of association between two or more variables is referred to as correlation.
Social psychologists	Social psychologists study the nature and causes of human social behavior, emphasizing on how people think and relate towards each other.
Loftus	Loftus works on human memory and how it can be changed by facts, ideas, suggestions and other forms of post-event information. One of her famous studies include the "car accident" study, which was an example of the misinformation effect.
Fundamental attribution error	The fundamental attribution error is the tendency for people to over-emphasize dispositional, or personality-based, explanations for behaviors observed in others while under-emphasizing the role and power of situational influences on the same behavior.
Social psychology	Social psychology is the study of the nature and causes of human social behavior, with an emphasis on how people think towards each other and how they relate to each other.
Romantic love	An intense, positive emotion that involves sexual attraction, feelings of caring, and the

belief that one is in love is romantic love.

Laboratory setting | Research setting in which the behavior of interest does not naturally occur is called a laboratory setting.

52

Go to **Cram101.com** for the Practice Tests for this Chapter.

Ego	In Freud's view the Ego serves to balance our primitive needs and our moral beliefs and taboos. Relying on experience, a healthy Ego provides the ability to adapt to reality and interact with the outside world.
Psychoanalytic	Freud's theory that unconscious forces act as determinants of personality is called psychoanalytic theory. The theory is a developmental theory characterized by critical stages of development.
Personality	Personality refers to the pattern of enduring characteristics that differentiates a person, the patterns of behaviors that make each individual unique.
Anna Freud	Anna Freud was a pioneer of child psychoanalysis. She popularized the notion that adolescence is a period that includes rapid mood fluctuation with enormous uncertainty about self.
Adler	Adler argued that human personality could be explained teleologically, separate strands dominated by the guiding purpose of the individual's unconscious self ideal to convert feelings of inferiority to superiority (or rather completeness). The desires of the self ideal were countered by social and ethical demands.
Sigmund Freud	Sigmund Freud was the founder of the psychoanalytic school, based on his theory that unconscious motives control much behavior, that particular kinds of unconscious thoughts and memories are the source of neurosis, and that neurosis could be treated through bringing these unconscious thoughts and memories to consciousness in psychoanalytic treatment.
Sullivan	Sullivan developed the Self System, a configuration of the personality traits developed in childhood and reinforced by positive affirmation and the security operations developed in childhood to avoid anxiety and threats to self-esteem.
Infancy	The developmental period that extends from birth to 18 or 24 months is called infancy.
Erik Erikson	Erik Erikson conceived eight stages of development, each confronting the individual with its own psychosocial demands, that continued into old age. Personality development, according to Erikson, takes place through a series of crises that must be overcome and internalized by the individual in preparation for the next developmental stage. Such crisis are not catastrophes but vulnerabilities.
Psychoanalyst	A psychoanalyst is a specially trained therapist who attempts to treat the individual by uncovering and revealing to the individual otherwise subconscious factors that are contributing to some undesirable behavior.
Theories	Theories are logically self-consistent models or frameworks describing the behavior of a certain natural or social phenomenon. They are broad explanations and predictions concerning phenomena of interest.
Questionnaire	A self-report method of data collection or clinical assessment method in which the individual being studied checks off items on a printed list, answers multiple-choice questions, or writes out answers to essay questions aimed at producing a selfdescription is called questionnaire.
Population	Population refers to all members of a well-defined group of organisms, events, or things.
Psychoanalysis	Psychoanalysis refers to the school of psychology that emphasizes the importance of unconscious motives and conflicts as determinants of human behavior. It was Freud's method of exploring human personality.
Trauma	Trauma refers to a severe physical injury or wound to the body caused by an external force, or a psychological shock having a lasting effect on mental life.
Attention	Attention is the cognitive process of selectively concentrating on one thing while ignoring other things. Psychologists have labeled three types of attention: sustained attention,

selective attention, and divided attention.

Empirical	Empirical means the use of working hypotheses which are capable of being disproved using observation or experiment.
Psychoanalytic theory	Psychoanalytic theory is a general term for approaches to psychoanalysis which attempt to provide a conceptual framework more-or-less independent of clinical practice rather than based on empirical analysis of clinical cases.
Psychotherapy	Psychotherapy is a set of techniques based on psychological principles intended to improve mental health, emotional or behavioral issues.
Neo-Freudian	The Neo-Freudian psychologists were those followers of Sigmund Freud who accepted the basic tenets of his theory of psychoanalysis but altered it in some way.
Karen Horney	Karen Horney, a neo-Freudian, deviated from orthodox Freudian analysis by emphasizing environmental and cultural, rather than biological, factors in neurosis.
Oedipus complex	The Oedipus complex is a concept developed by Sigmund Freud to explain the maturation of the infant boy through identification with the father and desire for the mother.
Innate	Innate behavior is not learned or influenced by the environment, rather, it is present or predisposed at birth.
Adaptation	Adaptation is a lowering of sensitivity to a stimulus following prolonged exposure to that stimulus. Behavioral adaptations are special ways a particular organism behaves to survive in its natural habitat.
Social role	Social role refers to expected behavior patterns associated with particular social positions.
Affect	A subjective feeling or emotional tone often accompanied by bodily expressions noticeable to others is called affect.
Self-actualization	Self-actualization (a term originated by Kurt Goldstein) is the instinctual need of a human to make the most of their unique abilities. Maslow described it as follows: Self Actualization is the intrinsic growth of what is already in the organism, or more accurately, of what the organism is.
Humanistic	Humanistic refers to any system of thought focused on subjective experience and human problems and potentials.
Free will	The idea that human beings are capable of freely making choices or decisions is free will.
Attitude	An enduring mental representation of a person, place, or thing that evokes an emotional response and related behavior is called attitude.
Allport	Allport was a trait theorist. Those traits he believed to predominate a person's personality were called central traits. Traits such that one could be indentifed by the trait, were referred to as cardinal traits. Central traits and cardinal traits are influenced by environmental factors.
Maslow	Maslow is mostly noted today for his proposal of a hierarchy of human needs which he often presented as a pyramid. Maslow was an instrumental player in the formation of the humanistic movement, also known as the third force in psychology.
Social psychologists	Social psychologists study the nature and causes of human social behavior, emphasizing on how people think and relate towards each other.
Inferiority complex	An inferiority complex is a feeling that one is inferior to others in some way. It is often unconscious, and is thought to drive afflicted individuals to overcompensate, resulting either in spectacular achievement or extreme antisocial behavior.

Jung	Jung was in some aspects a response to Sigmund Freud's psychoanalysis. He proposed and developed the concepts of the extroverted and introverted personality, archetypes, and the collective unconscious. His work has been influential in psychiatry and in the study of religion, literature, and related fields.
Society	The social sciences use the term society to mean a group of people that form a semi-closed (or semi-open) social system, in which most interactions are with other individuals belonging to the group.
Individual psychology	Alfred Adler's individual psychology approach views people as motivated by purposes and goals, being creators of their own lives .
Punishment	Punishment is the addtion of a stimulus that reduces the frequency of a response, or the removal of a stimulus that results in a reduction of the response.
Creativity	Creativity is the ability to think about something in novel and unusual ways and come up with unique solutions to problems. It involves divergent thinking, having many solutions or views to a problem.
Subjective experience	Subjective experience refers to reality as it is perceived and interpreted, not as it exists objectively.
Puberty	Puberty refers to the process of physical changes by which a child's body becomes an adult body capable of reproduction.
Socialization	Social rules and social relations are created, communicated, and changed in verbal and nonverbal ways creating social complexity useful in identifying outsiders and intelligent breeding partners. The process of learning these skills is called socialization.
Maladjustment	Maladjustment is the condition of being unable to adapt properly to your environment with resulting emotional instability.
Compensation	In personaility, compensation, according to Adler, is an effort to overcome imagined or real inferiorities by developing one's abilities.
Lesbian	A lesbian is a homosexual woman. They are women who are sexually and romantically attracted to other women.
Trait	An enduring personality characteristic that tends to lead to certain behaviors is called a trait. The term trait also means a genetically inherited feature of an organism.
Motivation	In psychology, motivation is the driving force (desire) behind all actions of an organism.
Fictional finalism	Adlerian Psychology assumes a central personality dynamic reflecting the growth and forward movement of life. It is a future-oriented striving toward an ideal goal of significance, superiority, success, or completion. The early childhood feeling of inferiority, for which one aims to compensate, leads to the creation of a fictional finalism which subjectively seems to promise total relief from the feeling of inferiority, future security, and success.
Defense mechanism	A Defense mechanism is a set of unconscious ways to protect one's personality from unpleasant thoughts and realities which may otherwise cause anxiety. The notion is an integral part of the psychoanalytic theory.
Repression	A defense mechanism, repression involves moving thoughts unacceptable to the ego into the unconscious, where they cannot be easily accessed.
Anti-social	Anti-social behavior is lacking in judgement and consideration for others, ranging from careless negligence to deliberately damaging activity, vandalism and graffiti for example.
Self-concept	Self-concept refers to domain-specific evaluations of the self where a domain may be academics, athletics, etc.

Go to **Cram101.com** for the Practice Tests for this Chapter.

Hippocampus	The hippocampus is a part of the brain located inside the temporal lobe. It forms a part of the limbic system and plays a part in memory and navigation.
Brain	The brain controls and coordinates most movement, behavior and homeostatic body functions such as heartbeat, blood pressure, fluid balance and body temperature. Functions of the brain are responsible for cognition, emotion, memory, motor learning and other sorts of learning. The brain is primarily made up of two types of cells: glia and neurons.
Schema	Schema refers to a way of mentally representing the world, such as a belief or an expectation, that can influence perception of persons, objects, and situations.
Personality inventory	A self-report questionnaire by which an examinee indicates whether statements assessing habitual tendencies apply to him or her is referred to as a personality inventory.
Correlation	A statistical technique for determining the degree of association between two or more variables is referred to as correlation.
Hypothesis	A specific statement about behavior or mental processes that is testable through research is a hypothesis.
Depression	In everyday language depression refers to any downturn in mood, which may be relatively transitory and perhaps due to something trivial. This is differentiated from Clinical depression which is marked by symptoms that last two weeks or more and are so severe that they interfere with daily living.
Paradigm	Paradigm refers to the set of practices that defines a scientific discipline during a particular period of time. It provides a framework from which to conduct research, it ensures that a certain range of phenomena, those on which the paradigm focuses, are explored thoroughly. Itmay also blind scientists to other, perhaps more fruitful, ways of dealing with their subject matter.
Maladaptive	In psychology, a behavior or trait is adaptive when it helps an individual adjust and function well within their social environment. A maladaptive behavior or trait is counterproductive to the individual.
Drug addiction	Drug addiction, or substance dependence is the compulsive use of drugs, to the point where the user has no effective choice but to continue use.
Alcoholism	A disorder that involves long-term, repeated, uncontrolled, compulsive, and excessive use of alcoholic beverages and that impairs the drinker's health and work and social relationships is called alcoholism.
Addiction	Addiction is an uncontrollable compulsion to repeat a behavior regardless of its consequences. Many drugs or behaviors can precipitate a pattern of conditions recognized as addiction, which include a craving for more of the drug or behavior, increased physiological tolerance to exposure, and withdrawal symptoms in the absence of the stimulus.
Suicide	Suicide behavior is rare in childhood but escalates in adolescence. The suicide rate increases in a linear fashion from adolescence through late adulthood.
Agoraphobia	An irrational fear of open, crowded places is called agoraphobia. Many people suffering from agoraphobia, however, are not afraid of the open spaces themselves, but of situations often associated with these spaces, such as social gatherings.
Social learning	Social learning is learning that occurs as a function of observing, retaining and replicating behavior observed in others. Although social learning can occur at any stage in life, it is thought to be particularly important during childhood, particularly as authority becomes important.
Learning	Learning is a relatively permanent change in behavior that results from experience. Thus, to

Go to **Cram101.com** for the Practice Tests for this Chapter.

attribute a behavioral change to learning, the change must be relatively permanent and must result from experience.

Bandura	Bandura is best known for his work on social learning theory or Social Cognitivism. His famous Bobo doll experiment illustrated that people learn from observing others.
Mischel	Mischel is known for his cognitive social learning model of personality that focuses on the specific cognitive variables that mediate the manner in which new experiences affect the individual.
Rotter	Rotter focused on the application of social learning theory (SLT) to clinical psychology. She introduced the ideas of learning from generalized expectancies of reinforcement and internal/external locus of control (self-initiated change versus change influenced by others). According to Rotter, health outcomes could be improved by the development of a sense of personal control over one's life.
Longitudinal research	Research that studies the same subjects over an extended period of time, usually several years or more, is called longitudinal research.
Masculinity	Masculinity is a culturally determined value reflecting the set of characteristics of maleness.
Femininity	Femininity is the set of characteristics defined by a culture for idealized females.
Longitudinal study	Longitudinal study is a type of developmental study in which the same group of participants is followed and measured for an extended period of time, often years.
Perception	Perception is the process of acquiring, interpreting, selecting, and organizing sensory information.
Locus of control	The place to which an individual attributes control over the receiving of reinforcers -either inside or outside the self is referred to as locus of control.
Ethnic identity	An enduring, basic aspect of the self that includes a sense of membership in an ethnic group and the attitudes and feelings related to that membership is called an ethnic identity.
Egocentrism	The inability to distinguish between one's own perspective and someone else's is referred to as egocentrism.
Narcissism	Narcissism is the pattern of thinking and behaving which involves infatuation and obsession with one's self to the exclusion of others.
Schachter	Schachter found that all emotions have approximately the same arousal pattern; variation is only in strength of the impulse and actions are largely dependent on our cognitive appraisal of the situation.
Autonomy	Autonomy is the condition of something that does not depend on anything else.
Evolution	Commonly used to refer to gradual change, evolution is the change in the frequency of alleles within a population from one generation to the next. This change may be caused by different mechanisms, including natural selection, genetic drift, or changes in population (gene flow).
Darwin	Darwin achieved lasting fame as originator of the theory of evolution through natural selection. His book Expression of Emotions in Man and Animals is generally considered the first text on comparative psychology.
Galton	Galton was one of the first experimental psychologists, and the founder of the field of Differential Psychology, which concerns itself with individual differences rather than on common trends. He created the statistical methods correlation and regression.
Individualism	Individualism refers to putting personal goals ahead of group goals and defining one's identity in terms of personal attributes rather than group memberships.

Extraversion	Extraversion, one of the big-five personailty traits, is marked by pronounced engagement with the external world. They are people who enjoy being with people, are full of energy, and often experience positive emotions.
Empathy	Empathy is the recognition and understanding of the states of mind, including beliefs, desires and particularly emotions of others without injecting your own.
Moral development	Development regarding rules and conventions about what people should do in their interactions with other people is called moral development.
Neurosis	Neurosis, any mental disorder that, although may cause distress, does not interfere with rational thought or the persons' ability to function.
Schizophrenia	Schizophrenia is characterized by persistent defects in the perception or expression of reality. A person suffering from untreated schizophrenia typically demonstrates grossly disorganized thinking, and may also experience delusions or auditory hallucinations
Construct	A generalized concept, such as anxiety or gravity, is a construct.
Insight	Insight refers to a sudden awareness of the relationships among various elements that had previously appeared to be independent of one another.
Sexual dysfunction	Sexual dysfunction or sexual malfunction is difficulty during any stage of the sexual act (which includes desire, arousal, orgasm, and resolution) that prevents the individual or couple from enjoying sexual activity.
Homosexual	Homosexual refers to a sexual orientation characterized by aesthetic attraction, romantic love, and sexual desire exclusively for members of the same sex or gender identity.
Friendship	The essentials of friendship are reciprocity and commitment between individuals who see themselves more or less as equals. Interaction between friends rests on a more equal power base than the interaction between children and adults.
Corporal punishment	Corporal punishment is the use of physical force with the intention of causing pain, but not injury.
Juvenile delinquency	Juvenile delinquency refers to a broad range of child and adolescent behaviors, including socially unacceptable behavior, status offenses, and criminal acts.
Reinforcement	In operant conditioning, reinforcement is any change in an environment that (a) occurs after the behavior, (b) seems to make that behavior re-occur more often in the future and (c) that reoccurence of behavior must be the result of the change.
Launching	The process in which youths move into adulthood and exit their family of origin is called launching. It can be a time to formulate life goals, to develop an identity, and to become more independent before joining with another person to form a new family.
Incest	Incest refers to sexual relations between close relatives, most often between daughter and father or between brother and sister.
Transference	Transference is a phenomenon in psychology characterized by unconscious redirection of feelings from one person to another.
Authoritarian	The term authoritarian is used to describe a style that enforces strong and sometimes oppressive measures against those in its sphere of influence, generally without attempts at gaining their consent.
Anxiety	Anxiety is a complex combination of the feeling of fear, apprehension and worry often accompanied by physical sensations such as palpitations, chest pain and/or shortness of breath.
Migraine	Migraine is a form of headache, usually very intense and disabling. It is a neurologic

Go to Cram101.com for the Practice Tests for this Chapter.

101

	disease.
Sperry	Sperry separated the corpus callosum, the area of the brain used to transfer signals between the right and left hemispheres, to treat epileptics. He then tested these patients with tasks that were known to be dependant on specific hemispheres of the brain and demonstrated that the two halves of the brain now had independent functions.
Hypnosis	Hypnosis is a psychological state whose existence and effects are strongly debated. Some believe that it is a state under which the subject's mind becomes so suggestible that the hypnotist, the one who induces the state, can establish communication with the subconscious mind of the subject and command behavior that the subject would not choose to perform in a conscious state.
Cognitive therapy	Cognitive therapy is a kind of psychotherapy used to treat depression, anxiety disorders, phobias, and other forms of mental disorder. It involves recognizing distorted thinking and learning how to replace it with more realistic thoughts and actions.
Creative self	According to Alfred Adler, the self-aware aspect of personality that strives to achieve its full potential is referred to as the creative self.
Determinism	Determinism is the philosophical proposition that every event, including human cognition and action, is causally determined by an unbroken chain of prior occurrences.
Self-esteem	Self-esteem refers to a person's subjective appraisal of himself or herself as intrinsically positive or negative to some degree.

Go to **Cram101.com** for the Practice Tests for this Chapter.
And, **NEVER** highlight a book again!

Adolescence	The period of life bounded by puberty and the assumption of adult responsibilities is adolescence.
Self-esteem	Self-esteem refers to a person's subjective appraisal of himself or herself as intrinsically positive or negative to some degree.
Infancy	The developmental period that extends from birth to 18 or 24 months is called infancy.
Generativity	Generativity refers to an adult's concern for and commitment to the well-being of future generations.
Stages	Stages represent relatively discrete periods of time in which functioning is qualitatively different from functioning at other periods.
Ego	In Freud's view the Ego serves to balance our primitive needs and our moral beliefs and taboos. Relying on experience, a healthy Ego provides the ability to adapt to reality and interact with the outside world.
Psychiatrist	A psychiatrist is a physician who specializes in the diagnosis and treatment of psychological disorders.
Icon	A mental representation of a visual stimulus that is held briefly in sensory memory is called icon.
Identity statuses	The states of ego development that depend on the presence or absence of crisis and commitment are called identity statuses.
Questionnaire	A self-report method of data collection or clinical assessment method in which the individual being studied checks off items on a printed list, answers multiple-choice questions, or writes out answers to essay questions aimed at producing a selfdescription is called questionnaire.
Attention	Attention is the cognitive process of selectively concentrating on one thing while ignoring other things. Psychologists have labeled three types of attention: sustained attention, selective attention, and divided attention.
Society	The social sciences use the term society to mean a group of people that form a semi-closed (or semi-open) social system, in which most interactions are with other individuals belonging to the group.
Psychoanalysis	Psychoanalysis refers to the school of psychology that emphasizes the importance of unconscious motives and conflicts as determinants of human behavior. It was Freud's method of exploring human personality.
Psychoanalytic	Freud's theory that unconscious forces act as determinants of personality is called psychoanalytic theory. The theory is a developmental theory characterized by critical stages of development.
Motivation	In psychology, motivation is the driving force (desire) behind all actions of an organism.
Adaptation	Adaptation is a lowering of sensitivity to a stimulus following prolonged exposure to that stimulus. Behavioral adaptations are special ways a particular organism behaves to survive in its natural habitat.
Personality	Personality refers to the pattern of enduring characteristics that differentiates a person, the patterns of behaviors that make each individual unique.
Psychosocial stages	Erikson's eight developmental stages through the life span, each defined by a conflict that must be resolved satisfactorily in order for healthy personality development to occur are called psychosocial stages.
Psychosocial	Erikson's psychosocial development describe eight developmental stages through which a

development	healthily developing human should pass from infancy to late adulthood. In each stage the person confronts, and hopefully masters, new challenges.
Erik Erikson	Erik Erikson conceived eight stages of development, each confronting the individual with its own psychosocial demands, that continued into old age. Personality development, according to Erikson, takes place through a series of crises that must be overcome and internalized by the individual in preparation for the next developmental stage. Such crisis are not catastrophes but vulnerabilities.
Critical thinking	Critical thinking is a mental process of analyzing or evaluating information, particularly statements or propositions that are offered as true.
Hysteria	Hysteria is a diagnostic label applied to a state of mind, one of unmanageable fear or emotional excesses. The fear is often centered on a body part, most often on an imagined problem with that body part.
Montessori	As an educational approach, the Montessori method's central focus is on the needs, talents, gifts, and special individuality of each child. Montessori practitioners believe children learn best in their own way at their own pace.
Life span	Life span refers to the upper boundary of life, the maximum number of years an individual can live. The maximum life span of human beings is about 120 years of age. Females live an average of 6 years longer than males.
Fetus	A fetus develops from the end of the 8th week of pregnancy (when the major structures have formed), until birth.
Autonomy	Autonomy is the condition of something that does not depend on anything else.
Psychosexual stages	In Freudian theory each child passes through five psychosexual stages. During each stage, the id focuses on a distinct erogenous zone on the body. Suffering from trauma during any of the first three stages may result in fixation in that stage. Freud related the resolutions of the stages with adult personalities and personality disorders.
Latency stage	Sigmund Freud suggested that the latency stage, age 6-10, this was a time of sexual latency, when the healthy child ceased all sexual interest and was vulnerable to trauma if he or she experienced sexuality.
Latency	In child development, latency refers to a phase of psychosexual development characterized by repression of sexual impulses. In learning theory, latency is the delay between stimulus (S) and response (R), which according to Hull depends on the strength of the association.
Psychosexual development	In psychodynamic theory, the process by which libidinal energy is expressed through different erogenous zones during different stages of development is called psychosexual development.
Trust versus mistrust	In Erikson's first stage of psychosexual development, trust versus mistrust, children do-or do not-come to trust that primary caregivers and the environment will meet their needs. The first year of life is the key time for the development of attachment.
Nurture	Nurture refers to the environmental influences on behavior due to nutrition, culture, socioeconomic status, and learning.
Socioeconomic Status	A family's socioeconomic status is based on family income, parental education level, parental occupation, and social status in the community. Those with high status often have more success in preparing their children for school because they have access to a wide range of resources.
Socioeconomic	Socioeconomic pertains to the study of the social and economic impacts of any product or service offering, market intervention or other activity on an economy as a whole and on the companies, organization and individuals who are its main economic actors.

Prototype	A concept of a category of objects or events that serves as a good example of the category is called a prototype.
Friendship	The essentials of friendship are reciprocity and commitment between individuals who see themselves more or less as equals. Interaction between friends rests on a more equal power base than the interaction between children and adults.
Autonomy versus shame and doubt	In Erikson's second stage of development, autonomy versus shame and doubt, which occurs in late infancy and toddlerhood, infants begin to discover that their behavior is their own.
Toddler	A toddler is a child between the ages of one and three years old. During this period, the child learns a great deal about social roles and develops motor skills; to toddle is to walk unsteadily.
Initiative versus guilt	Initiative versus guilt is Erikson's third stage of development, which occurs during the preschool years. As preschool children encounter a widening social world, they are challenged more than they were as infants.
Guilt	Guilt describes many concepts related to a negative emotion or condition caused by actions which are believed to be, morally wrong. According to Freud, the avoidance of guilt is the basis for moral behavior.
Superego	Frued's third psychic structure, which functions as a moral guardian and sets forth high standards for behavior is the superego.
Industry versus inferiority	Erikson's fourth stage of development, industry versus inferiority, develops in the elementary school years. Initiative brings children into contact with a new experiences. They direct their energy toward mastering knowledge and intellectual skills.
Puberty	Puberty refers to the process of physical changes by which a child's body becomes an adult body capable of reproduction.
Identity versus identity confusion	Identity versus identity confusion is Erikson's fifth developmental stage, which individuals experience during the adolescent years. At this time, individuals are faced with finding out who they are, what they re all about, and where they are going in life.
Identity crisis	Erikson coinded the term identity crisis: "...a psychosocial state or condition of disorientation and role confusion occurring especially in adolescents as a result of conflicting internal and external experiences, pressures, and expectations and often producing acute anxiety."
Personal identity	The portion of the self-concept that pertains to the self as a distinct, separate individual is called personal identity.
Role model	A person who serves as a positive example of desirable behavior is referred to as a role model.
Population	Population refers to all members of a well-defined group of organisms, events, or things.
Juvenile delinquent	An adolescent who breaks the law or engages in behavior that is considered illegal is referred to as a juvenile delinquent.
Social role	Social role refers to expected behavior patterns associated with particular social positions.
Generativity versus stagnation	Generativity versus stagnation is Erikson's term for the crisis of middle adulthood. The individual is characterized by the task of being productive and contributing to younger generations.
Integrity versus despair	Erikson's eighth and final stage of development is Integrity Versus Despair. In late adulthood individuals reflect on the past and either piece together a positive review or conclude that one's life has not been well spent.

Go to **Cram101.com** for the Practice Tests for this Chapter.

Punishment	Punishment is the addtion of a stimulus that reduces the frequency of a response, or the removal of a stimulus that results in a reduction of the response.
Psychoanalytic theory	Psychoanalytic theory is a general term for approaches to psychoanalysis which attempt to provide a conceptual framework more-or-less independent of clinical practice rather than based on empirical analysis of clinical cases.
Discrimination	In Learning theory, discrimination refers the ability to distinguish between a conditioned stimulus and other stimuli. It can be brought about by extensive training or differential reinforcement. In social terms, it is the denial of privileges to a person or a group on the basis of prejudice.
Ideology	An ideology can be thought of as a comprehensive vision, as a way of looking at things, as in common sense and several philosophical tendencies, or a set of ideas proposed by the dominant class of a society to all members of this society.
Conservation	Conservation refers to the recognition that basic properties of substances such as weight and mass remain the same even when transformations merely alter their appearance.
Evolution	Commonly used to refer to gradual change, evolution is the change in the frequency of alleles within a population from one generation to the next. This change may be caused by different mechanisms, including natural selection, genetic drift, or changes in population (gene flow).
Homosexual	Homosexual refers to a sexual orientation characterized by aesthetic attraction, romantic love, and sexual desire exclusively for members of the same sex or gender identity.
Wisdom	Wisdom is the ability to make correct judgments and decisions. It is an intangible quality gained through experience. Whether or not something is wise is determined in a pragmatic sense by its popularity, how long it has been around, and its ability to predict against future events.
Ethnic identity	An enduring, basic aspect of the self that includes a sense of membership in an ethnic group and the attitudes and feelings related to that membership is called an ethnic identity.
Acute	Acute means sudden, sharp, and abrupt. Usually short in duration.
Ethnic group	An ethnic group is a culture or subculture whose members are readily distinguishable by outsiders based on traits originating from a common racial, national, linguistic, or religious source. Members of an ethnic group are often presumed to be culturally or biologically similar, although this is not in fact necessarily the case.
Attitude	An enduring mental representation of a person, place, or thing that evokes an emotional response and related behavior is called attitude.
Interdependence	Interdependence is a dynamic of being mutually responsible to and dependent on others.
Cross-cultural studies	Cross-cultural studies are comparisons of a culture with one or more other cultures, which provides information about the degree to which behavior is similar across cultures or the degree to which it is culture specific .
Individuality	According to Cooper, individuality consists of two dimensions: self-assertion and separateness.
Syndrome	The term syndrome is the association of several clinically recognizable features, signs, symptoms, phenomena or characteristics which often occur together, so that the presence of one feature indicates the presence of the others.
Gender identity	Gender identity describes the gender with which a person identifies, but can also be used to refer to the gender that other people attribute to the individual on the basis of what they know from gender role indications.

Suppression	Suppression is the defense mechanism where a memory is deliberately forgotten.
Perception	Perception is the process of acquiring, interpreting, selecting, and organizing sensory information.
Ethnicity	Ethnicity refers to a characteristic based on cultural heritage, nationality characteristics, race, religion, and language.
Internalization	The developmental change from behavior that is externally controlled to behavior that is controlled by internal standards and principles is referred to as internalization.
Individualism	Individualism refers to putting personal goals ahead of group goals and defining one's identity in terms of personal attributes rather than group memberships.
Collectivism	Collectivism is an emphasis on the group, as opposed to the individual. It is syndrome of attitudes and behaviors based on the belief that the basic unit of survival lies within a group, not the individual.
Individualistic	Cultures have been classified as individualistic, which means having a set of values that give priority to personal goals rather than group goals.
Species	Species refers to a reproductively isolated breeding population.
Projection	Attributing one's own undesirable thoughts, impulses, traits, or behaviors to others is referred to as projection.
Penis	The penis is the external male copulatory organ and the external male organ of urination. In humans, the penis is homologous to the female clitoris, as it develops from the same embryonic structure. It is capable of erection for use in copulation.
Variance	The degree to which scores differ among individuals in a distribution of scores is the variance.
Self-actualization	Self-actualization (a term originated by Kurt Goldstein) is the instinctual need of a human to make the most of their unique abilities. Maslow described it as follows: Self Actualization is the intrinsic growth of what is already in the organism, or more accurately, of what the organism is.
Locus of control	The place to which an individual attributes control over the receiving of reinforcers -either inside or outside the self is referred to as locus of control.
Moral reasoning	Moral reasoning involves concepts of justice, whereas social conventional judgments are concepts of social organization.
Reasoning	Reasoning is the act of using reason to derive a conclusion from certain premises. There are two main methods to reach a conclusion,deductive reasoning and inductive reasoning.
Longitudinal study	Longitudinal study is a type of developmental study in which the same group of participants is followed and measured for an extended period of time, often years.
Personality test	A personality test aims to describe aspects of a person's character that remain stable across situations.
Masculinity	Masculinity is a culturally determined value reflecting the set of characteristics of maleness.
Marcia	Marcia argued that identity could be viewed as a structure of beliefs, abilities and past experiences regarding the self. Identity is a dynamic, not static structure. At least three aspects of the adolescent's development are important in identity formation: must be confident that they have parental support, must have an established sense of industry, and must be able to adopt a self-reflective stance toward the future.

Go to **Cram101.com** for the Practice Tests for this Chapter.

101

77

Empirical	Empirical means the use of working hypotheses which are capable of being disproved using observation or experiment.
Identity foreclosure	Identity foreclosure is Marcia's term for adolescents who have made a commitment but have not experienced a crisis.
Identity diffusion	Identity diffusion is Marcia's term for adolescents who have not yet experienced a crisis or made any commitments.
Survey	A method of scientific investigation in which a large sample of people answer questions about their attitudes or behavior is referred to as a survey.
Identity Achievement	Identity achievement is Marcia's term for an adolescent's having undergone a crisis and made a commitment.
Hypothesis	A specific statement about behavior or mental processes that is testable through research is a hypothesis.
Defense mechanism	A Defense mechanism is a set of unconscious ways to protect one's personality from unpleasant thoughts and realities which may otherwise cause anxiety. The notion is an integral part of the psychoanalytic theory.
Moral judgment	Making decisions about which actions are right and which are wrong is a moral judgment.
Authoritarian	The term authoritarian is used to describe a style that enforces strong and sometimes oppressive measures against those in its sphere of influence, generally without attempts at gaining their consent.
Psychodynamic	Most psychodynamic approaches are centered around the idea of a maladapted function developed early in life (usually childhood) which are at least in part unconscious. This maladapted function (a.k.a. defense mechanism) does not do well in place of a normal/healthy one.
Self-concept	Self-concept refers to domain-specific evaluations of the self where a domain may be academics, athletics, etc.
Anxiety	Anxiety is a complex combination of the feeling of fear, apprehension and worry often accompanied by physical sensations such as palpitations, chest pain and/or shortness of breath.
Authoritarian parents	Parents who are rigid in their rules and who demand obedience for the sake of obedience are called authoritarian parents.
Projective test	A projective test is a personality test designed to let a person respond to ambiguous stimuli, presumably revealing hidden emotions and internal conflicts. This is different from an "objective test" in which responses are analyzed according to a universal standard rather than an individual psychiatrist's judgement.
Need for Power	Need for Power is a term introduced by David McClelland referring to an individual's need to be in charge. There are two kinds of power, social and personal.
Femininity	Femininity is the set of characteristics defined by a culture for idealized females.
Personality inventory	A self-report questionnaire by which an examinee indicates whether statements assessing habitual tendencies apply to him or her is referred to as a personality inventory.
Positive correlation	A relationship between two variables in which both vary in the same direction is called a positive correlation.
Stage theory	Stage theory characterizes development by hypothesizing the existence of distinct, and often critical, periods of life. Each period follows one another in an orderly sequence.
Correlation	A statistical technique for determining the degree of association between two or more

variables is referred to as correlation.

Gender difference	A gender difference is a disparity between genders involving quality or quantity. Though some gender differences are controversial, they are not to be confused with sexist stereotypes.
Speciation	Speciation refers to the evolutionary process by which new biological species arise. There are three main ideas concerning the creation of new species, each based on the degree to which populations undergoing this process are geographically isolated from one another.
Kohut	Kohut was a pioneer in the fields of psychology and psychiatry. He established the school of Self Psychology as a branch of psychoanalysis. Where Freud empahasized guilt in the etiology of emotional disorders, Kohut saw shame as more central.

80

Go to **Cram101.com** for the Practice Tests for this Chapter.

Go to **Cram101.com** for the Practice Tests for this Chapter.
And, **NEVER** highlight a book again!

Insecure attachment	Insecure attachment occurs when infants either avoid the caregiver or show considerable resistance or ambivalence toward the caregiver.
Attachment style	Attachment style refers to the way a person typically interacts with significant others.
Attachment	Attachment is the tendency to seek closeness to another person and feel secure when that person is present.
Psychoanalytic theory	Psychoanalytic theory is a general term for approaches to psychoanalysis which attempt to provide a conceptual framework more-or-less independent of clinical practice rather than based on empirical analysis of clinical cases.
Psychoanalytic	Freud's theory that unconscious forces act as determinants of personality is called psychoanalytic theory. The theory is a developmental theory characterized by critical stages of development.
Personality	Personality refers to the pattern of enduring characteristics that differentiates a person, the patterns of behaviors that make each individual unique.
Insight	Insight refers to a sudden awareness of the relationships among various elements that had previously appeared to be independent of one another.
Stroke	A stroke occurs when the blood supply to a part of the brain is suddenly interrupted by occlusion, by hemorrhage, or other causes
Gender role	A cluster of behaviors that characterizes traditional female or male behaviors within a cultural setting is a gender role.
Theories	Theories are logically self-consistent models or frameworks describing the behavior of a certain natural or social phenomenon. They are broad explanations and predictions concerning phenomena of interest.
Stereotype	A stereotype is considered to be a group concept, held by one social group about another.They are often used in a negative or prejudicial sense and are frequently used to justify certain discriminatory behaviors. This allows powerful social groups to legitimize and protect their dominant position
Society	The social sciences use the term society to mean a group of people that form a semi-closed (or semi-open) social system, in which most interactions are with other individuals belonging to the group.
Self-esteem	Self-esteem refers to a person's subjective appraisal of himself or herself as intrinsically positive or negative to some degree.
Defense mechanism	A Defense mechanism is a set of unconscious ways to protect one's personality from unpleasant thoughts and realities which may otherwise cause anxiety. The notion is an integral part of the psychoanalytic theory.
Depression	In everyday language depression refers to any downturn in mood, which may be relatively transitory and perhaps due to something trivial. This is differentiated from Clinical depression which is marked by symptoms that last two weeks or more and are so severe that they interfere with daily living.
Persona	In Jungian archetypal psychology, the Persona is the mask or appearance one presents to the world. It may appear in dreams under various guises.
Psychiatrist	A psychiatrist is a physician who specializes in the diagnosis and treatment of psychological disorders.
Anxiety	Anxiety is a complex combination of the feeling of fear, apprehension and worry often accompanied by physical sensations such as palpitations, chest pain and/or shortness of

Go to Cram101.com for the Practice Tests for this Chapter.

	breath.
Adaptation	Adaptation is a lowering of sensitivity to a stimulus following prolonged exposure to that stimulus. Behavioral adaptations are special ways a particular organism behaves to survive in its natural habitat.
Psychoanalysis	Psychoanalysis refers to the school of psychology that emphasizes the importance of unconscious motives and conflicts as determinants of human behavior. It was Freud's method of exploring human personality.
Object relation	Object relation theory is the idea that the ego-self exists only in relation to other objects, which may be external or internal.
Cognition	The intellectual processes through which information is obtained, transformed, stored, retrieved, and otherwise used is cognition.
Emotion	An emotion is a mental states that arise spontaneously, rather than through conscious effort. They are often accompanied by physiological changes.
Shaping	The concept of reinforcing successive, increasingly accurate approximations to a target behavior is called shaping. The target behavior is broken down into a hierarchy of elemental steps, each step more sophisticated then the last. By successively reinforcing each of the the elemental steps, a form of differential reinforcement, until that step is learned while extinguishing the step below, the target behavior is gradually achieved.
Basic anxiety	Basic anxiety is a child's insecurity and doubt when a parent is indifferent, unloving, or disparaging. This anxiety, according to Horney, leads the child to a basic hostility toward his or her parents. The child may then become neurotic as an adult.
Karen Horney	Karen Horney, a neo-Freudian, deviated from orthodox Freudian analysis by emphasizing environmental and cultural, rather than biological, factors in neurosis.
Adler	Adler argued that human personality could be explained teleologically, separate strands dominated by the guiding purpose of the individual's unconscious self ideal to convert feelings of inferiority to superiority (or rather completeness). The desires of the self ideal were countered by social and ethical demands.
Psychoanalyst	A psychoanalyst is a specially trained therapist who attempts to treat the individual by uncovering and revealing to the individual otherwise subconscious factors that are contributing to some undesirable behavior.
Fixation	Fixation in abnormal psychology is the state where an individual becomes obsessed with an attachment to another human, animal or inanimate object. Fixation in vision refers to maintaining the gaze in a constant direction. .
Social psychology	Social psychology is the study of the nature and causes of human social behavior, with an emphasis on how people think towards each other and how they relate to each other.
Attitude	An enduring mental representation of a person, place, or thing that evokes an emotional response and related behavior is called attitude.
Jung	Jung was in some aspects a response to Sigmund Freud's psychoanalysis. He proposed and developed the concepts of the extroverted and introverted personality, archetypes, and the collective unconscious. His work has been influential in psychiatry and in the study of religion, literature, and related fields.
Motivation	In psychology, motivation is the driving force (desire) behind all actions of an organism.
Penis	The penis is the external male copulatory organ and the external male organ of urination. In humans, the penis is homologous to the female clitoris, as it develops from the same embryonic structure. It is capable of erection for use in copulation.

Go to **Cram101.com** for the Practice Tests for this Chapter.

Senses	The senses are systems that consist of a sensory cell type that respond to a specific kind of physical energy, and that correspond to a defined region within the brain where the signals are received and interpreted.
Punishment	Punishment is the addtion of a stimulus that reduces the frequency of a response, or the removal of a stimulus that results in a reduction of the response.
Friendship	The essentials of friendship are reciprocity and commitment between individuals who see themselves more or less as equals. Interaction between friends rests on a more equal power base than the interaction between children and adults.
Assertiveness	Assertiveness basically means the ability to express your thoughts and feelings in a way that clearly states your needs and keeps the lines of communication open with the other.
Coronary heart disease	Coronary heart disease is the end result of the accumulation of atheromatous plaques within the walls of the arteries that supply the myocardium (the muscle of the heart).
Epilepsy	Epilepsy is a chronic neurological condition characterized by recurrent unprovoked neural discharges. It is commonly controlled with medication, although surgical methods are used as well.
Asthma	Asthma is a complex disease characterized by bronchial hyperresponsiveness (BHR), inflammation, mucus production and intermittent airway obstruction.
Repression	A defense mechanism, repression involves moving thoughts unacceptable to the ego into the unconscious, where they cannot be easily accessed.
Self-worth	In psychology, self-esteem or self-worth refers to a person's subjective appraisal of himself or herself as intrinsically positive or negative to some degree.
Neurosis	Neurosis, any mental disorder that, although may cause distress, does not interfere with rational thought or the persons' ability to function.
Suicide	Suicide behavior is rare in childhood but escalates in adolescence. The suicide rate increases in a linear fashion from adolescence through late adulthood.
Substance abuse	Substance abuse refers to the overindulgence in and dependence on a stimulant, depressant, or other chemical substance, leading to effects that are detrimental to the individual's physical or mental health, or the welfare of others.
Mood disorder	A mood disorder is a condition where the prevailing emotional mood is distorted or inappropriate to the circumstances.
Projection	Attributing one's own undesirable thoughts, impulses, traits, or behaviors to others is referred to as projection.
Case study	A carefully drawn biography that may be obtained through interviews, questionnaires, and psychological tests is called a case study.
Self-image	A person's self-image is the mental picture, generally of a kind that is quite resistant to change, that depicts not only details that are potentially available to objective investigation by others, but also items that have been learned by that person about himself or herself.
Blind spot	In anatomy, the blind spot is the region of the retina where the optic nerve and blood vessels pass through to connect to the back of the eye. Since there are no light receptors there, a part of the field of vision is not perceived.
Rationalization	Rationalization is the process of constructing a logical justification for a decision that was originally arrived at through a different mental process. It is one of Freud's defense mechanisms.

Reasoning	Reasoning is the act of using reason to derive a conclusion from certain premises. There are two main methods to reach a conclusion,deductive reasoning and inductive reasoning.
Free association	In psychoanalysis, the uncensored uttering of all thoughts that come to mind is called free association.
Psychotherapy	Psychotherapy is a set of techniques based on psychological principles intended to improve mental health, emotional or behavioral issues.
Trait	An enduring personality characteristic that tends to lead to certain behaviors is called a trait. The term trait also means a genetically inherited feature of an organism.
Chromosome	The DNA which carries genetic information in biological cells is normally packaged in the form of one or more large macromolecules called a chromosome. Humans normally have 46.
Social role theory	The theory that small gender differences are magnified in perception by the contrasting social roles occupied by men and women is called social role theory.
Role theory	Role theory is a perspective that considers most of everyday activity to be living up to the roles, or expectations, of others. The central weakness of role theory is in describing and explaining deviant behavior.
Social role	Social role refers to expected behavior patterns associated with particular social positions.
Projective test	A projective test is a personality test designed to let a person respond to ambiguous stimuli, presumably revealing hidden emotions and internal conflicts. This is different from an "objective test" in which responses are analyzed according to a universal standard rather than an individual psychiatrist's judgement.
Empirical	Empirical means the use of working hypotheses which are capable of being disproved using observation or experiment.
Connectedness	Connectedness, according to Cooper, consists of two dimensions: mutuality and permeability. Connectedness involves processes that link the self to others, as seen in acknowledgment of, respect for, and responsiveness to others.
Empathy	Empathy is the recognition and understanding of the states of mind, including beliefs, desires and particularly emotions of others without injecting your own.
Nurture	Nurture refers to the environmental influences on behavior due to nutrition, culture, socioeconomic status, and learning.
Marcia	Marcia argued that identity could be viewed as a structure of beliefs, abilities and past experiences regarding the self. Identity is a dynamic, not static structure. At least three aspects of the adolescent's development are important in identity formation: must be confident that they have parental support, must have an established sense of industry, and must be able to adopt a self-reflective stance toward the future.
Masculinity	Masculinity is a culturally determined value reflecting the set of characteristics of maleness.
Femininity	Femininity is the set of characteristics defined by a culture for idealized females.
Homosexual	Homosexual refers to a sexual orientation characterized by aesthetic attraction, romantic love, and sexual desire exclusively for members of the same sex or gender identity.
Individualism	Individualism refers to putting personal goals ahead of group goals and defining one's identity in terms of personal attributes rather than group memberships.
Individualistic	Cultures have been classified as individualistic, which means having a set of values that give priority to personal goals rather than group goals.

Go to **Cram101.com** for the Practice Tests for this Chapter.

Collectivism	Collectivism is an emphasis on the group, as opposed to the individual. It is syndrome of attitudes and behaviors based on the belief that the basic unit of survival lies within a group, not the individual.
Collectivist	A person who defines the self in terms of relationships to other people and groups and gives priority to group goals is called collectivist.
Conformity	Conformity is the degree to which members of a group will change their behavior, views and attitudes to fit the views of the group. The group can influence members via unconscious processes or via overt social pressure on individuals.
Self-concept	Self-concept refers to domain-specific evaluations of the self where a domain may be academics, athletics, etc.
Life satisfaction	A person's attitudes about his or her overall life are referred to as life satisfaction.
Individualist	A person who defines the self in terms of personal traits and gives priority to personal goals is an individualist.
Attention	Attention is the cognitive process of selectively concentrating on one thing while ignoring other things. Psychologists have labeled three types of attention: sustained attention, selective attention, and divided attention.
Clinician	A health professional authorized to provide services to people suffering from one or more pathologies is a clinician.
Norms	In testing, standards of test performance that permit the comparison of one person's score on the test to the scores of others who have taken the same test are referred to as norms.
Immune system	The most important function of the human immune system occurs at the cellular level of the blood and tissues. The lymphatic and blood circulation systems are highways for specialized white blood cells. These cells include B cells, T cells, natural killer cells, and macrophages. All function with the primary objective of recognizing, attacking and destroying bacteria, viruses, cancer cells, and all substances seen as foreign.
Population	Population refers to all members of a well-defined group of organisms, events, or things.
Basic evil	According to Horney anything that parents do to frustrate the basic needs of their child and thus undermine the child 's feeling of security is considered basic evil.
Trauma	Trauma refers to a severe physical injury or wound to the body caused by an external force, or a psychological shock having a lasting effect on mental life.
Affective	Affective is the way people react emotionally, their ability to feel another living thing's pain or joy.
Longitudinal research	Research that studies the same subjects over an extended period of time, usually several years or more, is called longitudinal research.
Neuroticism	Eysenck's use of the term neuroticism (or Emotional Stability) was proposed as the dimension describing individual differences in the predisposition towards neurotic disorder.
Ego	In Freud's view the Ego serves to balance our primitive needs and our moral beliefs and taboos. Relying on experience, a healthy Ego provides the ability to adapt to reality and interact with the outside world.
Authoritative parents	Authoritative parents are strict and warm. Authoritative parents demand mature behavior but use reason rather than force in discipline.
Pathology	Pathology is the study of the processes underlying disease and other forms of illness, harmful abnormality, or dysfunction.

Narcissistic personality disorder	The narcissistic personality disorder a Cluster B (dramatic, emotional, or erratic) personality disorder. It is a life-long pattern of traits and behaviors which signify infatuation and obsession with one's self to the exclusion of all others and the egotistic and ruthless pursuit of one's gratification, dominance and ambition.
Personality disorder	A mental disorder characterized by a set of inflexible, maladaptive personality traits that keep a person from functioning properly in society is referred to as a personality disorder.
Borderline personality disorder	Borderline personality disorder is characterized by extreme 'black and white' thinking, mood swings, emotional reasoning, disrupted relationships and difficulty in functioning in a way society accepts as normal.
Construct	A generalized concept, such as anxiety or gravity, is a construct.
Secure attachment	With secure attachment, the infant uses a caregiver as a secure base from which to explore the environment. Ainsworth believes that secure attachment in the first year of life provides an important foundation for psychological development later in life.
Transference	Transference is a phenomenon in psychology characterized by unconscious redirection of feelings from one person to another.
Libido	Sigmund Freud suggested that libido is the instinctual energy or force that can come into conflict with the conventions of civilized behavior. Jung, condidered the libido as the free creative, or psychic, energy an individual has to put toward personal development, or individuation.
Paradigm	Paradigm refers to the set of practices that defines a scientific discipline during a particular period of time. It provides a framework from which to conduct research, it ensures that a certain range of phenomena, those on which the paradigm focuses, are explored thoroughly. Itmay also blind scientists to other, perhaps more fruitful, ways of dealing with their subject matter.
Affect	A subjective feeling or emotional tone often accompanied by bodily expressions noticeable to others is called affect.
Q-sort technique	The Q-sort technique is a standardized procedure forassessing the self-concept. It entails making ranked comparative judgments of statements about one's self.
Kohut	Kohut was a pioneer in the fields of psychology and psychiatry. He established the school of Self Psychology as a branch of psychoanalysis. Where Freud empahasized guilt in the etiology of emotional disorders, Kohut saw shame as more central.
Emotional abuse	There is no single accepted definition of emotional abuse which, like other forms of violence in a relationship, is based on power and domination.
Sexual abuse	Sexual abuse is a term used to describe non- consentual sexual relations between two or more parties which are considered criminally and/or morally offensive.
Illusion	An illusion is a distortion of a sensory perception.
Group dynamics	The term group dynamics implies that individual behaviors may differ depending on individuals' current or prospective connections to a sociological group.
Narcissism	Narcissism is the pattern of thinking and behaving which involves infatuation and obsession with one's self to the exclusion of others.
Mental disorder	Mental disorder refers to a disturbance in a person's emotions, drives, thought processes, or behavior that involves serious and relatively prolonged distress and/or impairment in ability to function, is not simply a normal response to some event or set of events in the person's environment.

Domestic violence	Domestic violence is any violence between current or former partners in an intimate relationship, wherever and whenever the violence occurs. The violence may include physical, sexual, emotional or financial abuse.
Narcissist	The narcissist has an unhealthily high self-esteem. For the narcissist, self-worth is the belief that he/she is superior to his/her fellow humans; it is not enough to be "okay" or "pretty good," the narcissist can only feel worthwhile by experiencing him/herself as the "best".
Laboratory setting	Research setting in which the behavior of interest does not naturally occur is called a laboratory setting.
Infancy	The developmental period that extends from birth to 18 or 24 months is called infancy.
Bowlby	Bowlby, a developmental psychologist of the psychoanalytic tradition, was responsible for much of the early research conducted on attachment in humans. He identified three stages of separation: protest, despair, and detachment.
Cognitive development	The process by which a child's understanding of the world changes as a function of age and experience is called cognitive development.
Temperament	Temperament refers to a basic, innate disposition to change behavior. The activity level is an important dimension of temperament.
Genetics	Genetics is the science of genes, heredity, and the variation of organisms.
Erik Erikson	Erik Erikson conceived eight stages of development, each confronting the individual with its own psychosocial demands, that continued into old age. Personality development, according to Erikson, takes place through a series of crises that must be overcome and internalized by the individual in preparation for the next developmental stage. Such crisis are not catastrophes but vulnerabilities.
Conduct disorder	Conduct disorder is the psychiatric diagnostic category for the occurrence of multiple delinquent activities over a 6-month period. These behaviors include truancy, running away, fire setting, cruelty to animals, breaking and entering, and excessive fighting.
Avoidant attachment	A type of insecure attachment characterized by apparent indifference to the leave-takings of, and reunions with, an attachment figure is referred to as avoidant attachment.
Sperling	Sperling has studied cognitive psychology and was a prominent researcher in memory. He is responsible for the concept of iconic memory.
Secure attachment style	In Bartholomew's model, a secure attachment style is characterized by high self-esteem and high interpersonal trust. It is usually described as the ideal and most successful attachment style.
Ambivalence	The simultaneous holding of strong positive and negative emotional attitudes toward the same situation or person is called ambivalence.
Representative sample	Representative sample refers to a sample of participants selected from the larger population in such a way that important subgroups within the population are included in the sample in the same proportions as they are found in the larger population.
Psychopathology	Psychopathology refers to the field concerned with the nature and development of mental disorders.
Developmental psychologist	A psychologist interested in human growth and development from conception until death is referred to as a developmental psychologist.
Social cognition	Social cognition is the name for both a branch of psychology that studies the cognitive processes involved in social interaction, and an umbrella term for the processes themselves.

95

	It uses the tools and assumptions of cognitive psychology to study how people understand themselves and others in society and social situations.
Correlation	A statistical technique for determining the degree of association between two or more variables is referred to as correlation.
Maladaptive	In psychology, a behavior or trait is adaptive when it helps an individual adjust and function well within their social environment. A maladaptive behavior or trait is counterproductive to the individual.
Oedipus complex	The Oedipus complex is a concept developed by Sigmund Freud to explain the maturation of the infant boy through identification with the father and desire for the mother.

Go to **Cram101.com** for the Practice Tests for this Chapter.

Raymond Cattell	Raymond Cattell proposed that 16 factors underlie human personality. He called these 16 factors source traits because he believed that they provide the underlying source for the surface behaviors that we think of as personality.
Personality	Personality refers to the pattern of enduring characteristics that differentiates a person, the patterns of behaviors that make each individual unique.
Construct	A generalized concept, such as anxiety or gravity, is a construct.
Allport	Allport was a trait theorist. Those traits he believed to predominate a person's personality were called central traits. Traits such that one could be indentifed by the trait, were referred to as cardinal traits. Central traits and cardinal traits are influenced by environmental factors.
Trait	An enduring personality characteristic that tends to lead to certain behaviors is called a trait. The term trait also means a genetically inherited feature of an organism.
Individual differences	Individual differences psychology studies the ways in which individual people differ in their behavior. This is distinguished from other aspects of psychology in that although psychology is ostensibly a study of individuals, modern psychologists invariably study groups.
Theories	Theories are logically self-consistent models or frameworks describing the behavior of a certain natural or social phenomenon. They are broad explanations and predictions concerning phenomena of interest.
Questionnaire	A self-report method of data collection or clinical assessment method in which the individual being studied checks off items on a printed list, answers multiple-choice questions, or writes out answers to essay questions aimed at producing a selfdescription is called questionnaire.
Factor analysis	Factor analysis is a statistical technique that originated in psychometrics. The objective is to explain the most of the variability among a number of observable random variables in terms of a smaller number of unobservable random variables called factors.
Conscientiou-ness	Conscientiousness is one of the dimensions of the five-factor model of personality and individual differences involving being organized, thorough, and reliable as opposed to careless, negligent, and unreliable.
Agreeableness	Agreeableness, one of the big-five personality traits, reflects individual differences in concern with cooperation and social harmony. It is the degree individuals value getting along with others.
Extraversion	Extraversion, one of the big-five personailty traits, is marked by pronounced engagement with the external world. They are people who enjoy being with people, are full of energy, and often experience positive emotions.
Neuroticism	Eysenck's use of the term neuroticism (or Emotional Stability) was proposed as the dimension describing individual differences in the predisposition towards neurotic disorder.
Big five	The big five factors of personality are Openness to experience, Conscientiousness, Extraversion, Agreeableness, and Emotional Stability.
Analogy	An analogy is a comparison between two different things, in order to highlight some form of similarity. Analogy is the cognitive process of transferring information from a particular subject to another particular subject.
Personality trait	According to the Diagnostic and Statistical Manual of the American Psychiatric Association, a personality trait is a "prominent aspect of personality that is exhibited in a wide range of important social and personal contexts. ...".
Neurotransmitter	A neurotransmitter is a chemical that is used to relay, amplify and modulate electrical

signals between a neurons and another cell.

Paradigm	Paradigm refers to the set of practices that defines a scientific discipline during a particular period of time. It provides a framework from which to conduct research, it ensures that a certain range of phenomena, those on which the paradigm focuses, are explored thoroughly. Itmay also blind scientists to other, perhaps more fruitful, ways of dealing with their subject matter.
Learning	Learning is a relatively permanent change in behavior that results from experience. Thus, to attribute a behavioral change to learning, the change must be relatively permanent and must result from experience.
Trait theory	According to trait theory, personality can be broken down into a limited number of traits, which are present in each individual to a greater or lesser degree. This approach is highly compatible with the quantitative psychometric approach to personality testing.
Humanistic	Humanistic refers to any system of thought focused on subjective experience and human problems and potentials.
Five-factor model	The five-factor model of personality proposes that there are five universal dimensions of personality: Neuroticism, Extraversion, Openness, Conscientiousness, and Agreeableness.
Superego	Frued's third psychic structure, which functions as a moral guardian and sets forth high standards for behavior is the superego.
Central nervous system	The vertebrate central nervous system consists of the brain and spinal cord.
Nervous system	The body's electrochemical communication circuitry, made up of billions of neurons is a nervous system.
Reinforcement	In operant conditioning, reinforcement is any change in an environment that (a) occurs after the behavior, (b) seems to make that behavior re-occur more often in the future and (c) that reoccurence of behavior must be the result of the change.
Empathy	Empathy is the recognition and understanding of the states of mind, including beliefs, desires and particularly emotions of others without injecting your own.
Sublimation	Sublimation is a coping mechanism. It refers to rechanneling sexual or aggressive energy into pursuits that society considers acceptable or admirable.
Instinct	Instinct is the word used to describe inherent dispositions towards particular actions. They are generally an inherited pattern of responses or reactions to certain kinds of situations.
Archetype	The archetype is a concept of psychologist Carl Jung. They are innate prototypes for ideas, which may subsequently become involved in the interpretation of observed phenomena. A group of memories and interpretations closely associated with an archetype is called a complex.
Attention	Attention is the cognitive process of selectively concentrating on one thing while ignoring other things. Psychologists have labeled three types of attention: sustained attention, selective attention, and divided attention.
Jung	Jung was in some aspects a response to Sigmund Freud's psychoanalysis. He proposed and developed the concepts of the extroverted and introverted personality, archetypes, and the collective unconscious. His work has been influential in psychiatry and in the study of religion, literature, and related fields.
Adler	Adler argued that human personality could be explained teleologically, separate strands dominated by the guiding purpose of the individual's unconscious self ideal to convert feelings of inferiority to superiority (or rather completeness). The desires of the self ideal were countered by social and ethical demands.

Go to **Cram101.com** for the Practice Tests for this Chapter.

Maslow	Maslow is mostly noted today for his proposal of a hierarchy of human needs which he often presented as a pyramid. Maslow was an instrumental player in the formation of the humanistic movement, also known as the third force in psychology.
Compensation	In personaility, compensation, according to Adler, is an effort to overcome imagined or real inferiorities by developing one's abilities.
Society	The social sciences use the term society to mean a group of people that form a semi-closed (or semi-open) social system, in which most interactions are with other individuals belonging to the group.
Nurture	Nurture refers to the environmental influences on behavior due to nutrition, culture, socioeconomic status, and learning.
Self-actualization	Self-actualization (a term originated by Kurt Goldstein) is the instinctual need of a human to make the most of their unique abilities. Maslow described it as follows: Self Actualization is the intrinsic growth of what is already in the organism, or more accurately, of what the organism is.
Ego	In Freud's view the Ego serves to balance our primitive needs and our moral beliefs and taboos. Relying on experience, a healthy Ego provides the ability to adapt to reality and interact with the outside world.
Kant	Kant held that all known objects are phenomena of consciousness and not realities of the mind. But, the known object is not a mere bundle of sensations for it includes unsensational characteristics or manifestation of a priori principles. He insisted that the scientist and the philosopher approached nature with certain implicit principles, and Kant saw his task to be that of finding and making explicit these principles.
Central trait	Gordon Allport delineated different kinds of traits, which he also called dispositions. A Central trait is basic to an individual's personality, while secondary traits are more peripheral. Common traits are those recognized within a culture and thus may vary from culture to culture. Cardinal traits are those by which an individual may be strongly recognized.
Schizophrenia	Schizophrenia is characterized by persistent defects in the perception or expression of reality. A person suffering from untreated schizophrenia typically demonstrates grossly disorganized thinking, and may also experience delusions or auditory hallucinations
Affect	A subjective feeling or emotional tone often accompanied by bodily expressions noticeable to others is called affect.
Tact	The word tact, another of Skinner's intentionally "nonsense" words, comes from the notion of the child's making "conTACT" with the nonverbal environment. The tact is verbal behavior that is under the control of the nonverbal environment and includes nouns, actions, adjectives, pronouns, relations, and others.
Social learning	Social learning is learning that occurs as a function of observing, retaining and replicating behavior observed in others. Although social learning can occur at any stage in life, it is thought to be particularly important during childhood, particularly as authority becomes important.
Humanistic theories	Humanistic theories focus attention on the whole, unique person, especially on the person's conscious understanding of his or her self and the world.
Premise	A premise is a statement presumed true within the context of a discourse, especially of a logical argument.
Prejudice	Prejudice in general, implies coming to a judgment on the subject before learning where the preponderance of the evidence actually lies, or formation of a judgement without direct

Go to **Cram101.com** for the Practice Tests for this Chapter.

experience.

Adaptation	Adaptation is a lowering of sensitivity to a stimulus following prolonged exposure to that stimulus. Behavioral adaptations are special ways a particular organism behaves to survive in its natural habitat.
Heredity	Heredity is the transfer of characteristics from parent to offspring through their genes.
Stages	Stages represent relatively discrete periods of time in which functioning is qualitatively different from functioning at other periods.
Humanistic psychology	Humanistic psychology refers to the school of psychology that focuses on the uniqueness of human beings and their capacity for choice, growth, and psychological health.
Humanistic movement	The humanistic movement places emphasis on a person's capacity for personal growth, freedom to choose a destiny, and positive qualities.
Psychoanalysis	Psychoanalysis refers to the school of psychology that emphasizes the importance of unconscious motives and conflicts as determinants of human behavior. It was Freud's method of exploring human personality.
Animal model	An animal model usually refers to a non-human animal with a disease that is similar to a human condition.
Motivation	In psychology, motivation is the driving force (desire) behind all actions of an organism.
John Watson	John Watson, the father of behaviorism, developed the term "Behaviorism" as a name for his proposal to revolutionize the study of human psychology in order to put it on a firm experimental footing.
Skinner	Skinner conducted research on shaping behavior through positive and negative reinforcement, and demonstrated operant conditioning, a technique which he developed in contrast with classical conditioning.
Attitude	An enduring mental representation of a person, place, or thing that evokes an emotional response and related behavior is called attitude.
Social influence	Social influence is when the actions or thoughts of individual(s) are changed by other individual(s). Peer pressure is an example of social influence.
Sigmund Freud	Sigmund Freud was the founder of the psychoanalytic school, based on his theory that unconscious motives control much behavior, that particular kinds of unconscious thoughts and memories are the source of neurosis, and that neurosis could be treated through bringing these unconscious thoughts and memories to consciousness in psychoanalytic treatment.
Phobia	A persistent, irrational fear of an object, situation, or activity that the person feels compelled to avoid is referred to as a phobia.
Intuition	Quick, impulsive thought that does not make use of formal logic or clear reasoning is referred to as intuition.
Gestalt psychology	According to Gestalt psychology, people naturally organize their perceptions according to certain patterns. The tendency is to organize perceptions into wholes and to integrate separate stimuli into meaningful patterns.
Infancy	The developmental period that extends from birth to 18 or 24 months is called infancy.
Clinical psychology	Clinical psychology is involved in the diagnosis, assessment, and treatment of patients with mental or behavioral disorders, and conducts research in these various areas.
Social psychology	Social psychology is the study of the nature and causes of human social behavior, with an emphasis on how people think towards each other and how they relate to each other.

Empirical	Empirical means the use of working hypotheses which are capable of being disproved using observation or experiment.
Psychopathology	Psychopathology refers to the field concerned with the nature and development of mental disorders.
Stimulus	A change in an environmental condition that elicits a response is a stimulus.
Population	Population refers to all members of a well-defined group of organisms, events, or things.
Temperament	Temperament refers to a basic, innate disposition to change behavior. The activity level is an important dimension of temperament.
Shyness	A tendency to avoid others plus uneasiness and strain when socializing is called shyness.
Reasoning	Reasoning is the act of using reason to derive a conclusion from certain premises. There are two main methods to reach a conclusion,deductive reasoning and inductive reasoning.
Mischel	Mischel is known for his cognitive social learning model of personality that focuses on the specific cognitive variables that mediate the manner in which new experiences affect the individual.
Psychoanalyst	A psychoanalyst is a specially trained therapist who attempts to treat the individual by uncovering and revealing to the individual otherwise subconscious factors that are contributing to some undesirable behavior.
Affective	Affective is the way people react emotionally, their ability to feel another living thing's pain or joy.
Individual traits	Personality traits that define a person's unique individual qualities are called individual traits.
Common traits	Common traits, according to Allport, are personality characteristics that are shared by most members of a particular culture or grouping.
Creativity	Creativity is the ability to think about something in novel and unusual ways and come up with unique solutions to problems. It involves divergent thinking, having many solutions or views to a problem.
Research method	The scope of the research method is to produce some new knowledge. This, in principle, can take three main forms: Exploratory research; Constructive research; and Empirical research.
Idiographic	An idiographic investigation studies the characteristics of an individual in depth.
Nomothetic	Nomothetic measures are contrasted to ipsative or idiothetic measures, where nomothetic measures are measures that can be taken directly by an outside observer, such as weight or how many times a particular behavior occurs, and ipsative measures are self-reports such as a rank-ordered list of preferences.
Reliability	Reliability means the extent to which a test produces a consistent , reproducible score .
Inference	Inference is the act or process of drawing a conclusion based solely on what one already knows.
Graphology	Graphology is the study of handwriting and its connection to behavior, and related data points. Critics cite the lack of supporting empirical evidence as a reason to not use it. Supporters point to the anecdotal evidence of thousands of positive testimonials, as a reason to use it.
Validity	The extent to which a test measures what it is intended to measure is called validity.
Social psychologists	Social psychologists study the nature and causes of human social behavior, emphasizing on how people think and relate towards each other.

Go to **Cram101.com** for the Practice Tests for this Chapter.

Homosexuality	Homosexuality refers to a sexual orientation characterized by aesthetic attraction, romantic love, and sexual desire exclusively for members of the same sex or gender identity.
Homosexual	Homosexual refers to a sexual orientation characterized by aesthetic attraction, romantic love, and sexual desire exclusively for members of the same sex or gender identity.
Sexual orientation	Sexual orientation refers to the sex or gender of people who are the focus of a person's amorous or erotic desires, fantasies, and spontaneous feelings, the gender(s) toward which one is primarily "oriented".
Ideology	An ideology can be thought of as a comprehensive vision, as a way of looking at things, as in common sense and several philosophical tendencies, or a set of ideas proposed by the dominant class of a society to all members of this society.
Lesbian	A lesbian is a homosexual woman. They are women who are sexually and romantically attracted to other women.
Rape	Rape is a crime where the victim is forced into sexual activity, in particular sexual penetration, against his or her will.
Impression management	Impression management is the process through which people try to control the impressions other people form of them.
Correlation	A statistical technique for determining the degree of association between two or more variables is referred to as correlation.
Altruism	Altruism is being helpful to other people with little or no interest in being rewarded for one's efforts. This is distinct from merely helping others.
Survey	A method of scientific investigation in which a large sample of people answer questions about their attitudes or behavior is referred to as a survey.
Group dynamics	The term group dynamics implies that individual behaviors may differ depending on individuals' current or prospective connections to a sociological group.
Ingroup	An ingroup is a social group towards which an individual feels loyalty and respect, usually due to membership in the group. This loyalty often manifests itself as an ingroup bias.
Goethe	Goethe argued that laws could not be created by pure rationalism, since geography and history shaped habits and patterns. This stood in sharp contrast to the prevailing Enlightenment view that reason was sufficient to create well-ordered societies and good laws.
Insight	Insight refers to a sudden awareness of the relationships among various elements that had previously appeared to be independent of one another.
Cardinal trait	A cardinal trait is Gordon Allport's name for a personal quality that is so strong a part of a person's personality, that he or she may become identified with that trait.
Perception	Perception is the process of acquiring, interpreting, selecting, and organizing sensory information.
Psychoanalytic	Freud's theory that unconscious forces act as determinants of personality is called psychoanalytic theory. The theory is a developmental theory characterized by critical stages of development.
Hypothesis	A specific statement about behavior or mental processes that is testable through research is a hypothesis.

Conscientiou-ness	Conscientiousness is one of the dimensions of the five-factor model of personality and individual differences involving being organized, thorough, and reliable as opposed to careless, negligent, and unreliable.
Superego	Frued's third psychic structure, which functions as a moral guardian and sets forth high standards for behavior is the superego.
Trait	An enduring personality characteristic that tends to lead to certain behaviors is called a trait. The term trait also means a genetically inherited feature of an organism.
Introversion	A personality trait characterized by intense imagination and a tendency to inhibit impulses is called introversion.
Agreeableness	Agreeableness, one of the big-five personality traits, reflects individual differences in concern with cooperation and social harmony. It is the degree individuals value getting along with others.
Empathy	Empathy is the recognition and understanding of the states of mind, including beliefs, desires and particularly emotions of others without injecting your own.
Attitude	An enduring mental representation of a person, place, or thing that evokes an emotional response and related behavior is called attitude.
Abstract principles	Concepts and ideas isolated from specific examples and concrete situations are referrd to as abstract principles.
Trait profile	A graph of the scores obtained on several personality traits is a trait profile.
Personality	Personality refers to the pattern of enduring characteristics that differentiates a person, the patterns of behaviors that make each individual unique.
Heritability	Heritability It is that proportion of the observed variation in a particular phenotype within a particular population, that can be attributed to the contribution of genotype. In other words: it measures the extent to which differences between individuals in a population are due their being different genetically.
Extraversion	Extraversion, one of the big-five personailty traits, is marked by pronounced engagement with the external world. They are people who enjoy being with people, are full of energy, and often experience positive emotions.
Normative	The term normative is used to describe the effects of those structures of culture which regulate the function of social activity.
Theories	Theories are logically self-consistent models or frameworks describing the behavior of a certain natural or social phenomenon. They are broad explanations and predictions concerning phenomena of interest.
Motives	Needs or desires that energize and direct behavior toward a goal are motives.
Big five	The big five factors of personality are Openness to experience, Conscientiousness, Extraversion, Agreeableness, and Emotional Stability.
Factor analysis	Factor analysis is a statistical technique that originated in psychometrics. The objective is to explain the most of the variability among a number of observable random variables in terms of a smaller number of unobservable random variables called factors.
Correlation	A statistical technique for determining the degree of association between two or more variables is referred to as correlation.
Correlation coefficient	Correlation coefficient refers to a number from +1.00 to -1.00 that expresses the direction and extent of the relationship between two variables. The closer to 1, the stronger the relationship. The sign, + or -, indicates the direction.

Go to **Cram101.com** for the Practice Tests for this Chapter.

Positive correlation	A relationship between two variables in which both vary in the same direction is called a positive correlation.
Personality test	A personality test aims to describe aspects of a person's character that remain stable across situations.
Adaptation	Adaptation is a lowering of sensitivity to a stimulus following prolonged exposure to that stimulus. Behavioral adaptations are special ways a particular organism behaves to survive in its natural habitat.
Psychosis	Psychosis is a generic term for mental states in which the components of rational thought and perception are severely impaired. Persons experiencing a psychosis may experience hallucinations, hold paranoid or delusional beliefs, demonstrate personality changes and exhibit disorganized thinking. This is usually accompanied by features such as a lack of insight into the unusual or bizarre nature of their behavior, difficulties with social interaction and impairments in carrying out the activities of daily living.
Heredity	Heredity is the transfer of characteristics from parent to offspring through their genes.
Predisposition	Predisposition refers to an inclination or diathesis to respond in a certain way, either inborn or acquired. In abnormal psychology, it is a factor that lowers the ability to withstand stress and inclines the individual toward pathology.
Maladjustment	Maladjustment is the condition of being unable to adapt properly to your environment with resulting emotional instability.
Personality trait	According to the Diagnostic and Statistical Manual of the American Psychiatric Association, a personality trait is a "prominent aspect of personality that is exhibited in a wide range of important social and personal contexts. ...".
Affect	A subjective feeling or emotional tone often accompanied by bodily expressions noticeable to others is called affect.
Biological predisposition	The genetic readiness of animals and humans to perform certain behaviors is a biological predisposition.
Variable	A variable refers to a measurable factor, characteristic, or attribute of an individual or a system.
Raymond Cattell	Raymond Cattell proposed that 16 factors underlie human personality. He called these 16 factors source traits because he believed that they provide the underlying source for the surface behaviors that we think of as personality.
Insight	Insight refers to a sudden awareness of the relationships among various elements that had previously appeared to be independent of one another.
Goethe	Goethe argued that laws could not be created by pure rationalism, since geography and history shaped habits and patterns. This stood in sharp contrast to the prevailing Enlightenment view that reason was sufficient to create well-ordered societies and good laws.
Research method	The scope of the research method is to produce some new knowledge. This, in principle, can take three main forms: Exploratory research; Constructive research; and Empirical research.
Projective test	A projective test is a personality test designed to let a person respond to ambiguous stimuli, presumably revealing hidden emotions and internal conflicts. This is different from an "objective test" in which responses are analyzed according to a universal standard rather than an individual psychiatrist's judgement.
Thorndike	Thorndike worked in animal behavior and the learning process leading to the theory of connectionism. Among his most famous contributions were his research on cats escaping from puzzle boxes, and his formulation of the Law of Effect.

Go to **Cram101.com** for the Practice Tests for this Chapter.

Maslow	Maslow is mostly noted today for his proposal of a hierarchy of human needs which he often presented as a pyramid. Maslow was an instrumental player in the formation of the humanistic movement, also known as the third force in psychology.
Intelligence test	An intelligence test is a standardized means of assessing a person's current mental ability, for example, the Stanford-Binet test and the Wechsler Adult Intelligence Scale.
Culture-fair	An intelligence test that does not discriminate against members of any minority group is called culture-fair.
American Psychological Association	The American Psychological Association is a professional organization representing psychology in the US. The mission statement is to "advance psychology as a science and profession and as a means of promoting health, education , and human welfare".
Allport	Allport was a trait theorist. Those traits he believed to predominate a person's personality were called central traits. Traits such that one could be indentifed by the trait, were referred to as cardinal traits. Central traits and cardinal traits are influenced by environmental factors.
Basic research	Basic research has as its primary objective the advancement of knowledge and the theoretical understanding of the relations among variables . It is exploratory and often driven by the researcher's curiosity, interest or hunch.
Psychological test	Psychological test refers to a standardized measure of a sample of a person's behavior.
Individual differences	Individual differences psychology studies the ways in which individual people differ in their behavior. This is distinguished from other aspects of psychology in that although psychology is ostensibly a study of individuals, modern psychologists invariably study groups.
Empirical	Empirical means the use of working hypotheses which are capable of being disproved using observation or experiment.
Questionnaire	A self-report method of data collection or clinical assessment method in which the individual being studied checks off items on a printed list, answers multiple-choice questions, or writes out answers to essay questions aimed at producing a selfdescription is called questionnaire.
Population	Population refers to all members of a well-defined group of organisms, events, or things.
Neuroticism	Eysenck's use of the term neuroticism (or Emotional Stability) was proposed as the dimension describing individual differences in the predisposition towards neurotic disorder.
Depression	In everyday language depression refers to any downturn in mood, which may be relatively transitory and perhaps due to something trivial. This is differentiated from Clinical depression which is marked by symptoms that last two weeks or more and are so severe that they interfere with daily living.
Anxiety	Anxiety is a complex combination of the feeling of fear, apprehension and worry often accompanied by physical sensations such as palpitations, chest pain and/or shortness of breath.
Innate	Innate behavior is not learned or influenced by the environment, rather, it is present or predisposed at birth.
Validity	The extent to which a test measures what it is intended to measure is called validity.
Ego	In Freud's view the Ego serves to balance our primitive needs and our moral beliefs and taboos. Relying on experience, a healthy Ego provides the ability to adapt to reality and interact with the outside world.

Go to **Cram101.com** for the Practice Tests for this Chapter.

Motivation	In psychology, motivation is the driving force (desire) behind all actions of an organism.
Surface trait	A surface trait is Cattell's name for observable qualities of personality, such as those used to describe a friend.
Source traits	Cattell's name for the traits that make up the most basic personality structure and causes of behavior is source traits.
Variance	The degree to which scores differ among individuals in a distribution of scores is the variance.
Punishment	Punishment is the addtion of a stimulus that reduces the frequency of a response, or the removal of a stimulus that results in a reduction of the response.
Guilt	Guilt describes many concepts related to a negative emotion or condition caused by actions which are believed to be, morally wrong. According to Freud, the avoidance of guilt is the basis for moral behavior.
Five-factor model	The five-factor model of personality proposes that there are five universal dimensions of personality: Neuroticism, Extraversion, Openness, Conscientiousness, and Agreeableness.
Introvert	Introvert refers to a person whose attention is focused inward; a shy, reserved, timid person.
Paranoid	The term paranoid is typically used in a general sense to signify any self-referential delusion, or more specifically, to signify a delusion involving the fear of persecution.
Psychoanalytic theory	Psychoanalytic theory is a general term for approaches to psychoanalysis which attempt to provide a conceptual framework more-or-less independent of clinical practice rather than based on empirical analysis of clinical cases.
Psychoanalytic	Freud's theory that unconscious forces act as determinants of personality is called psychoanalytic theory. The theory is a developmental theory characterized by critical stages of development.
Neurosis	Neurosis, any mental disorder that, although may cause distress, does not interfere with rational thought or the persons' ability to function.
Impulse control	Deferred gratification is the ability of a person to wait for things they want. This trait is critical for life success. Those who lack this trait are said to suffer from poor impulse control, and often become criminals, as they are unwilling to work and wait for their paycheck.
Temperament	Temperament refers to a basic, innate disposition to change behavior. The activity level is an important dimension of temperament.
Learning	Learning is a relatively permanent change in behavior that results from experience. Thus, to attribute a behavioral change to learning, the change must be relatively permanent and must result from experience.
Fluid intelligence	Mental flexibility in the ability to reason abstractly is called fluid intelligence. Fluid intelligence tends to decline around middle adulthood.
Crystallized intelligence	One's lifetime of intellectual achievement, as and shown largely through vocabulary and knowledge of world affairs is called crystallized intelligence.
Working Memory	Working memory is the collection of structures and processes in the brain used for temporarily storing and manipulating information. Working memory consists of both memory for items that are currently being processed, and components governing attention and directing the processing itself.
Brain	The brain controls and coordinates most movement, behavior and homeostatic body functions

such as heartbeat, blood pressure, fluid balance and body temperature. Functions of the brain are responsible for cognition, emotion, memory, motor learning and other sorts of learning. The brain is primarily made up of two types of cells: glia and neurons.

Cognition	The intellectual processes through which information is obtained, transformed, stored, retrieved, and otherwise used is cognition.
Genetics	Genetics is the science of genes, heredity, and the variation of organisms.
Eugenics	The field concerned with improving the hereditary qualities of the human race through social control of mating and reproduction is called eugenics.
Shaping	The concept of reinforcing successive, increasingly accurate approximations to a target behavior is called shaping. The target behavior is broken down into a hierarchy of elemental steps, each step more sophisticated then the last. By successively reinforcing each of the the elemental steps, a form of differential reinforcement, until that step is learned while extinguishing the step below, the target behavior is gradually achieved.
Kagan	The work of Kagan supports the concept of an inborn, biologically based temperamental predisposition to severe anxiety.
Attention	Attention is the cognitive process of selectively concentrating on one thing while ignoring other things. Psychologists have labeled three types of attention: sustained attention, selective attention, and divided attention.
Primary reinforcement	The use of reinforcers that are innately or biologically satisfying is called primary reinforcement.
Reinforcement	In operant conditioning, reinforcement is any change in an environment that (a) occurs after the behavior, (b) seems to make that behavior re-occur more often in the future and (c) that reoccurence of behavior must be the result of the change.
Self-assertion	Self-assertion refers to a direct, honest expression of feelings and desires.
Social support	Social Support is the physical and emotional comfort given by family, friends, co-workers and others. Research has identified three main types of social support: emotional, practical, sharing points of view.
Clinician	A health professional authorized to provide services to people suffering from one or more pathologies is a clinician.
Life space	Life space, according to Lewin, is the sum total of the psychological facts of an individual.
Mayer	Mayer developed the concept of emotional intelligence with Peter Salovey. He is one of the authors of the Mayer-Salovey-Caruso Emotional Intelligence Test, and has developed a new, integrated framework for personality psychology, known as the Systems Framework for Pesronality Psychology.
Lewin	Lewin ranks as one of the pioneers of social psychology, as one of the founders of group dynamics and as one of the most eminent representatives of Gestalt psychology.
Idiographic	An idiographic investigation studies the characteristics of an individual in depth.
Nomothetic	Nomothetic measures are contrasted to ipsative or idiothetic measures, where nomothetic measures are measures that can be taken directly by an outside observer, such as weight or how many times a particular behavior occurs, and ipsative measures are self-reports such as a rank-ordered list of preferences.
Psychosomatic	A psychosomatic illness is one with physical manifestations and perhaps a supposed psychological cause. It is often diagnosed when any known or identifiable physical cause was excluded by medical examination.

Stimulus	A change in an environmental condition that elicits a response is a stimulus.
Variability	Statistically, variability refers to how much the scores in a distribution spread out, away from the mean.
Self-esteem	Self-esteem refers to a person's subjective appraisal of himself or herself as intrinsically positive or negative to some degree.
Fraternal twins	Fraternal twins usually occur when two fertilized eggs are implanted in the uterine wall at the same time. The two eggs form two zygotes, and these twins are therefore also known as dizygotic. Dizygotic twins are no more similar genetically than any siblings.
Identical twins	Identical twins occur when a single egg is fertilized to form one zygote (monozygotic) but the zygote then divides into two separate embryos. The two embryos develop into foetuses sharing the same womb. Monozygotic twins are genetically identical unless there has been a mutation in development, and they are almost always the same gender.
Cyril Burt	Cyril Burt was controversial for his conclusions that genetics substantially influence mental and behavioral traits.
Shyness	A tendency to avoid others plus uneasiness and strain when socializing is called shyness.
Job satisfaction	A person's attitudes and feelings about his or her job and facets of the job is called job satisfaction.
Obedience	Obedience is the willingness to follow the will of others. Humans have been shown to be surprisingly obedient in the presence of perceived legitimate authority figures, as demonstrated by the Milgram experiment in the 1960s.
Five-factor theory	The five-factor theory of personality proposes that there are five universal dimensions of personality: Neuroticism, Extraversion, Openness, Conscientiousness, and Agreeableness.
Assertiveness	Assertiveness basically means the ability to express your thoughts and feelings in a way that clearly states your needs and keeps the lines of communication open with the other.
Altruism	Altruism is being helpful to other people with little or no interest in being rewarded for one's efforts. This is distinct from merely helping others.
Emotion	An emotion is a mental states that arise spontaneously, rather than through conscious effort. They are often accompanied by physiological changes.

Evolutionary psychology	Evolutionary psychology proposes that cognition and behavior can be better understood in light of evolutionary history.
Motives	Needs or desires that energize and direct behavior toward a goal are motives.
Empathy	Empathy is the recognition and understanding of the states of mind, including beliefs, desires and particularly emotions of others without injecting your own.
Evolutionary theory	Evolutionary theory is concerned with heritable variability rather than behavioral variations. Natural selection requirements: (1) natural variability within a species must exist, (2) only some individual differences are heritable, and (3) natural selection only takes place when there is an interaction between the inborn attributes of organisms and the environment in which they live.
Trait	An enduring personality characteristic that tends to lead to certain behaviors is called a trait. The term trait also means a genetically inherited feature of an organism.
Predisposition	Predisposition refers to an inclination or diathesis to respond in a certain way, either inborn or acquired. In abnormal psychology, it is a factor that lowers the ability to withstand stress and inclines the individual toward pathology.
Introversion	A personality trait characterized by intense imagination and a tendency to inhibit impulses is called introversion.
Extraversion	Extraversion, one of the big-five personailty traits, is marked by pronounced engagement with the external world. They are people who enjoy being with people, are full of energy, and often experience positive emotions.
Introvert	Introvert refers to a person whose attention is focused inward; a shy, reserved, timid person.
Heredity	Heredity is the transfer of characteristics from parent to offspring through their genes.
Neurotransmitter	A neurotransmitter is a chemical that is used to relay, amplify and modulate electrical signals between a neurons and another cell.
Dopamine	Dopamine is critical to the way the brain controls our movements and is a crucial part of the basal ganglia motor loop. It is commonly associated with the 'pleasure system' of the brain, providing feelings of enjoyment and reinforcement to motivate us to do, or continue doing, certain activities.
Brain	The brain controls and coordinates most movement, behavior and homeostatic body functions such as heartbeat, blood pressure, fluid balance and body temperature. Functions of the brain are responsible for cognition, emotion, memory, motor learning and other sorts of learning. The brain is primarily made up of two types of cells: glia and neurons.
Personality	Personality refers to the pattern of enduring characteristics that differentiates a person, the patterns of behaviors that make each individual unique.
Emotion	An emotion is a mental states that arise spontaneously, rather than through conscious effort. They are often accompanied by physiological changes.
Theories	Theories are logically self-consistent models or frameworks describing the behavior of a certain natural or social phenomenon. They are broad explanations and predictions concerning phenomena of interest.
Neuroticism	Eysenck's use of the term neuroticism (or Emotional Stability) was proposed as the dimension describing individual differences in the predisposition towards neurotic disorder.
Anxiety	Anxiety is a complex combination of the feeling of fear, apprehension and worry often accompanied by physical sensations such as palpitations, chest pain and/or shortness of

Go to **Cram101.com** for the Practice Tests for this Chapter.

	breath.
Temperament	Temperament refers to a basic, innate disposition to change behavior. The activity level is an important dimension of temperament.
Schizophrenia	Schizophrenia is characterized by persistent defects in the perception or expression of reality. A person suffering from untreated schizophrenia typically demonstrates grossly disorganized thinking, and may also experience delusions or auditory hallucinations
Nonconformity	Nonconformity occurs when individuals know what people around them expect but do not use those expectations to guide their behavior.
Psychoticism	Psychoticism is one of the three traits used by the psychologist Hans Eysenck in his P-E-N model of personality. High levels of this trait were believed by Eysenck to be linked to increased vulnerability to psychoses such as schizophrenia.
Creativity	Creativity is the ability to think about something in novel and unusual ways and come up with unique solutions to problems. It involves divergent thinking, having many solutions or views to a problem.
Genetic code	The genetic code is a set of rules, which maps DNA sequences to proteins in the living cell, and is employed in the process of protein synthesis. Nearly all living things use the same genetic code, called the standard genetic code, although a few organisms use minor variations of the standard code.
Gene	A gene is an ultramicroscopic area of the chromosome. It is the smallest physical unit of the DNA molecule that carries a piece of hereditary information.
Evolution	Commonly used to refer to gradual change, evolution is the change in the frequency of alleles within a population from one generation to the next. This change may be caused by different mechanisms, including natural selection, genetic drift, or changes in population (gene flow).
Nurture	Nurture refers to the environmental influences on behavior due to nutrition, culture, socioeconomic status, and learning.
Individual differences	Individual differences psychology studies the ways in which individual people differ in their behavior. This is distinguished from other aspects of psychology in that although psychology is ostensibly a study of individuals, modern psychologists invariably study groups.
Adaptation	Adaptation is a lowering of sensitivity to a stimulus following prolonged exposure to that stimulus. Behavioral adaptations are special ways a particular organism behaves to survive in its natural habitat.
Punishment	Punishment is the addtion of a stimulus that reduces the frequency of a response, or the removal of a stimulus that results in a reduction of the response.
Depression	In everyday language depression refers to any downturn in mood, which may be relatively transitory and perhaps due to something trivial. This is differentiated from Clinical depression which is marked by symptoms that last two weeks or more and are so severe that they interfere with daily living.
Addiction	Addiction is an uncontrollable compulsion to repeat a behavior regardless of its consequences. Many drugs or behaviors can precipitate a pattern of conditions recognized as addiction, which include a craving for more of the drug or behavior, increased physiological tolerance to exposure, and withdrawal symptoms in the absence of the stimulus.
Natural selection	Natural selection is a process by which biological populations are altered over time, as a result of the propagation of heritable traits that affect the capacity of individual organisms to survive and reproduce.
Species	Species refers to a reproductively isolated breeding population.

Go to **Cram101.com** for the Practice Tests for this Chapter.

Learning	Learning is a relatively permanent change in behavior that results from experience. Thus, to attribute a behavioral change to learning, the change must be relatively permanent and must result from experience.
Child development	Scientific study of the processes of change from conception through adolescence is called child development.
Infancy	The developmental period that extends from birth to 18 or 24 months is called infancy.
Paradigm	Paradigm refers to the set of practices that defines a scientific discipline during a particular period of time. It provides a framework from which to conduct research, it ensures that a certain range of phenomena, those on which the paradigm focuses, are explored thoroughly. Itmay also blind scientists to other, perhaps more fruitful, ways of dealing with their subject matter.
Personality psychology	Personality psychology is a branch of psychology which studies personality and individual difference processes. One emphasis in personality psychology is on trying to create a coherent picture of a person and all his or her major psychological processes.
Human nature	Human nature is the fundamental nature and substance of humans, as well as the range of human behavior that is believed to be invariant over long periods of time and across very different cultural contexts.
Dualism	Dualism is a set of beliefs which begins with the claim that the mental and the physical have a fundamentally different nature. It is contrasted with varying kinds of monism, including materialism and phenomenalism. Dualism is one answer to the mind-body problem.
Population	Population refers to all members of a well-defined group of organisms, events, or things.
Insight	Insight refers to a sudden awareness of the relationships among various elements that had previously appeared to be independent of one another.
Darwin	Darwin achieved lasting fame as originator of the theory of evolution through natural selection. His book Expression of Emotions in Man and Animals is generally considered the first text on comparative psychology.
Innate	Innate behavior is not learned or influenced by the environment, rather, it is present or predisposed at birth.
Prepared learning	Prepared learning is a concept that suggests certain associations can be learned more readily than others because this ability has been adaptive for the organism.
Altruism	Altruism is being helpful to other people with little or no interest in being rewarded for one's efforts. This is distinct from merely helping others.
Motivation	In psychology, motivation is the driving force (desire) behind all actions of an organism.
Attachment	Attachment is the tendency to seek closeness to another person and feel secure when that person is present.
Physical attractiveness	Physical attractiveness is the perception of an individual as physically beautiful by other people.
Testosterone	Testosterone is a steroid hormone from the androgen group. It is the principal male sex hormone and the "original" anabolic steroid.
Estrogen	Estrogen is a group of steroid compounds that function as the primary female sex hormone. They are produced primarily by developing follicles in the ovaries, the corpus luteum and the placenta.
Hormone	A hormone is a chemical messenger from one cell (or group of cells) to another. The best known are those produced by endocrine glands, but they are produced by nearly every organ

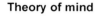

	system. The function of hormones is to serve as a signal to the target cells; the action of the hormone is determined by the pattern of secretion and the signal transduction of the receiving tissue.
Hume	Hume was the ultimate skeptic, reducing matter, mind, religion, and science to a matter of sense impressions and memories. He was a strong empiricist.
Hypothesis	A specific statement about behavior or mental processes that is testable through research is a hypothesis.
Questionnaire	A self-report method of data collection or clinical assessment method in which the individual being studied checks off items on a printed list, answers multiple-choice questions, or writes out answers to essay questions aimed at producing a selfdescription is called questionnaire.
Homosexual	Homosexual refers to a sexual orientation characterized by aesthetic attraction, romantic love, and sexual desire exclusively for members of the same sex or gender identity.
Gender difference	A gender difference is a disparity between genders involving quality or quantity. Though some gender differences are controversial, they are not to be confused with sexist stereotypes.
Secure attachment	With secure attachment, the infant uses a caregiver as a secure base from which to explore the environment. Ainsworth believes that secure attachment in the first year of life provides an important foundation for psychological development later in life.
Contact comfort	A hypothethetical primary drive to seek physical comfort through contact with another is called contact comfort.
Fight-or-flight	The fight-or-flight response, also called the "acute stress response", was first described by Walter Cannon. Animals react to threats with a general discharge of the sympathetic nervous system. In layman's terms, an animal has two options when faced with danger. They can either face the threat, or they can avoid the threat.
Oxytocin	Oxytocin is synthesized in magnocellular neurosecretory cells in the hypothalamus and released by the posterior lobe of the pituitary gland. It is involved in the facilitation of birth and breastfeeding as well as in bonding.
Homosexuality	Homosexuality refers to a sexual orientation characterized by aesthetic attraction, romantic love, and sexual desire exclusively for members of the same sex or gender identity.
Uterus	The uterus or womb is the major female reproductive organ. The main function of the uterus is to accept a fertilized ovum which becomes implanted into the endometrium, and derives nourishment from blood vessels which develop exclusively for this purpose.
Antisocial personality disorder	A disorder in which individuals tend to display no regard for the moral and ethical rules of society or the rights of others is called antisocial personality disorder.
Personality disorder	A mental disorder characterized by a set of inflexible, maladaptive personality traits that keep a person from functioning properly in society is referred to as a personality disorder.
Alcoholism	A disorder that involves long-term, repeated, uncontrolled, compulsive, and excessive use of alcoholic beverages and that impairs the drinker's health and work and social relationships is called alcoholism.
Theory of mind	A theory of mind considers the nature of mind, and its structure and processes
Kahneman	Kahneman is famous for collaboration with Amos Tversky and others in establishing a cognitive basis for common human errors using heuristics and in developing prospect theory.
Tversky	Tversky was a pioneer of cognitive science. With Kahneman, he originated prospect theory to

128

explain irrational human economic choices.

Framing	Framing refers to the way information is presented so as to emphasize either a potential gain or a potential loss as the outcome.
Authoritarian	The term authoritarian is used to describe a style that enforces strong and sometimes oppressive measures against those in its sphere of influence, generally without attempts at gaining their consent.
Heritability	Heritability It is that proportion of the observed variation in a particular phenotype within a particular population, that can be attributed to the contribution of genotype. In other words: it measures the extent to which differences between individuals in a population are due their being different genetically.
Attitude	An enduring mental representation of a person, place, or thing that evokes an emotional response and related behavior is called attitude.
Ego	In Freud's view the Ego serves to balance our primitive needs and our moral beliefs and taboos. Relying on experience, a healthy Ego provides the ability to adapt to reality and interact with the outside world.
Hippocrates	Hippocrates was an ancient Greek physician, commonly regarded as one of the most outstanding figures in medicine of all time; he has been called "the father of medicine."
Humors	The four humors were four fluids that were thought to permeate the body and influence its health. The concept was developed by ancient Greek thinkers around 400 BC and was directly linked with another popular theory of the four elements. Paired qualities were associated with each humour and its season.
Kagan	The work of Kagan supports the concept of an inborn, biologically based temperamental predisposition to severe anxiety.
Longitudinal study	Longitudinal study is a type of developmental study in which the same group of participants is followed and measured for an extended period of time, often years.
Attention	Attention is the cognitive process of selectively concentrating on one thing while ignoring other things. Psychologists have labeled three types of attention: sustained attention, selective attention, and divided attention.
Big five	The big five factors of personality are Openness to experience, Conscientiousness, Extraversion, Agreeableness, and Emotional Stability.
Variable	A variable refers to a measurable factor, characteristic, or attribute of an individual or a system.
Social support	Social Support is the physical and emotional comfort given by family, friends, co-workers and others. Research has identified three main types of social support: emotional, practical, sharing points of view.
Superego	Frued's third psychic structure, which functions as a moral guardian and sets forth high standards for behavior is the superego.
Adler	Adler argued that human personality could be explained teleologically, separate strands dominated by the guiding purpose of the individual's unconscious self ideal to convert feelings of inferiority to superiority (or rather completeness). The desires of the self ideal were countered by social and ethical demands.
Sympathetic	The sympathetic nervous system activates what is often termed the "fight or flight response". It is an automatic regulation system, that is, one that operates without the intervention of conscious thought.

Guthrie	The theory of learning proposed by Guthrie was based on one principle, Contiguity : A combination of stimuli which has accompanied a movement will on its recurrence tend to be followed by that movement. Prediction of behavior will always be probabilistic.
Sullivan	Sullivan developed the Self System, a configuration of the personality traits developed in childhood and reinforced by positive affirmation and the security operations developed in childhood to avoid anxiety and threats to self-esteem.
Phenotype	The phenotype of an individual organism is either its total physical appearance and constitution, or a specific manifestation of a trait, such as size or eye color, that varies between individuals. Phenotype is determined to some extent by genotype, or by the identity of the alleles that an individual carries at one or more positions on the chromosomes.
Genotype	The genotype is the specific genetic makeup of an individual, usually in the form of DNA. It codes for the phenotype of that individual. Any given gene will usually cause an observable change in an organism, known as the phenotype.
Hippocampus	The hippocampus is a part of the brain located inside the temporal lobe. It forms a part of the limbic system and plays a part in memory and navigation.
Physiology	The study of the functions and activities of living cells, tissues, and organs and of the physical and chemical phenomena involved is referred to as physiology.
Receptor	A sensory receptor is a structure that recognizes a stimulus in the internal or external environment of an organism. In response to stimuli the sensory receptor initiates sensory transduction by creating graded potentials or action potentials in the same cell or in an adjacent one.
Phineas Gage	As a result of an injury to his brain, Phineas Gage reportedly had significant changes in personality and temperament, which provided some of the first evidence that specific parts of the brain, particularly the frontal lobes, might be involved in specific psychological processes dealing with emotion, personality and problem solving.
Harlow	Harlow and his famous wire and cloth surrogate mother monkey studies demonstrated that the need for affection created a stronger bond between mother and infant than did physical needs. He also found that the more discrimination problems the monkeys solved, the better they became at solving them.
Cerebral cortex	The cerebral cortex is the outermost layer of the cerebrum and has a grey color. It is made up of four lobes and it is involved in many complex brain functions including memory, perceptual awareness, "thinking", language and consciousness. The cerebral cortex receives sensory information from many different sensory organs eg: eyes, ears, etc. and processes the information.
Correlation	A statistical technique for determining the degree of association between two or more variables is referred to as correlation.
Gray matter	Gray matter is a category of nervous tissue with many nerve cell bodies and few myelinated axons. Generally, gray matter can be understood as the parts of the brain responsible for information processing; whereas, white matter is responsible for information transmission. In addition, gray matter does not have a myelin sheath and does not regenerate after injury unlike white matter.
Prefrontal cortex	The prefrontal cortex is the anterior part of the frontal lobes of the brain, lying in front of the motor and associative areas. It has been implicated in planning complex cognitive behaviors, personality expression and moderating correct social behavior. The prefrontal cortex continues to develop until around age 6.
Right hemisphere	The brain is divided into left and right cerebral hemispheres. The right hemisphere of the

cortex controls the left side of the body.

Frontal lobe	The frontal lobe comprises four major folds of cortical tissue: the precentral gyrus, superior gyrus and the middle gyrus of the frontal gyri, the inferior frontal gyrus. It has been found to play a part in impulse control, judgement, language, memory, motor function, problem solving, sexual behavior, socialization and spontaneity.
Gyrus	A gyrus is a ridge on the cerebral cortex. It is generally surrounded by one or more sulci.
Mere exposure effect	The mere exposure effect is a psychological artifact well known to advertisers: people express undue liking for things merely because they are familiar with them. This effect has been nicknamed the "familiarity breeds liking" effect.
Cerebral hemisphere	Either of the two halves that make up the cerebrum is referred to as a cerebral hemisphere. The hemispheres operate together, linked by the corpus callosum, a very large bundle of nerve fibers, and also by other smaller commissures.
Left hemisphere	The left hemisphere of the cortex controls the right side of the body, coordinates complex movements, and, in 95% of people, controls the production of speech and written language.
Dissociation	Dissociation is a psychological state or condition in which certain thoughts, emotions, sensations, or memories are separated from the rest.
Amygdala	Located in the brain's medial temporal lobe, the almond-shaped amygdala is believed to play a key role in the emotions. It forms part of the limbic system and is linked to both fear responses and pleasure. Its size is positively correlated with aggressive behavior across species.
Phobia	A persistent, irrational fear of an object, situation, or activity that the person feels compelled to avoid is referred to as a phobia.
Central nervous system	The vertebrate central nervous system consists of the brain and spinal cord.
Nervous system	The body's electrochemical communication circuitry, made up of billions of neurons is a nervous system.
Epinephrine	Epinephrine is a hormone and a neurotransmitter. Epinephrine plays a central role in the short-term stress reaction—the physiological response to threatening or exciting conditions. It is secreted by the adrenal medulla. When released into the bloodstream, epinephrine binds to multiple receptors and has numerous effects throughout the body.
Serotonin	Serotonin, a neurotransmitter, is believed to play an important part of the biochemistry of depression, bipolar disorder and anxiety. It is also believed to be influential on sexuality and appetite.
Amino acid	Amino acid is the basic structural building unit of proteins. They form short polymer chains called peptides or polypeptides which in turn form structures called proteins.
Peptides	Peptides are the family of molecules formed from the linking, in a defined order, of various amino acids.
Emotional intelligence	The expression emotional intelligence indicates a kind of intelligence or skill that involves the ability to perceive, assess and positively influence one's own and other people's emotions.
Mayer	Mayer developed the concept of emotional intelligence with Peter Salovey. He is one of the authors of the Mayer-Salovey-Caruso Emotional Intelligence Test, and has developed a new, integrated framework for personality psychology, known as the Systems Framework for Pesronality Psychology.

Classical conditioning	Classical conditioning is a simple form of learning in which an organism comes to associate or anticipate events. A neutral stimulus comes to evoke the response usually evoked by a natural or unconditioned stimulus by being paired repeatedly with the unconditioned stimulus.
Conditioned response	A conditioned response is the response to a stimulus that occurs when an animal has learned to associate the stimulus with a certain positive or negative effect.
Conditioning	Conditioning describes the process by which behaviors can be learned or modified through interaction with the environment.
Pavlov	Pavlov first described the phenomenon now known as classical conditioning in experiments with dogs.
Stimulus	A change in an environmental condition that elicits a response is a stimulus.
Sensation	Sensation is the first stage in the chain of biochemical and neurologic events that begins with the impinging of a stimulus upon the receptor cells of a sensory organ, which then leads to perception, the mental state that is reflected in statements like "I see a uniformly blue wall."
Ascending reticular activating system	Ascending reticular activating system are the afferent fibers running through the reticular formation that influence physiological arousal.
Reticular activating system	The reticular activating system is the part of the brain believed to be the center of arousal and motivation. It is situated between the brain stem and the central nervous system (CNS).
Senses	The senses are systems that consist of a sensory cell type that respond to a specific kind of physical energy, and that correspond to a defined region within the brain where the signals are received and interpreted.
Electrode	Any device used to electrically stimulate nerve tissue or to record its activity is an electrode.
Personality test	A personality test aims to describe aspects of a person's character that remain stable across situations.
Latency	In child development, latency refers to a phase of psychosexual development characterized by repression of sexual impulses. In learning theory, latency is the delay between stimulus (S) and response (R), which according to Hull depends on the strength of the association.
Limbic system	The limbic system is a group of brain structures that are involved in various emotions such as aggression, fear, pleasure and also in the formation of memory. The limbic system affects the endocrine system and the autonomic nervous system. It consists of several subcortical structures located around the thalamus.
Defense mechanism	A Defense mechanism is a set of unconscious ways to protect one's personality from unpleasant thoughts and realities which may otherwise cause anxiety. The notion is an integral part of the psychoanalytic theory.
Pathology	Pathology is the study of the processes underlying disease and other forms of illness, harmful abnormality, or dysfunction.
Conditioned emotional response	Conditioned emotional response refers to an emotional response that has been linked to a previously non-emotional stimulus by classical conditioning.
Reinforcement	In operant conditioning, reinforcement is any change in an environment that (a) occurs after the behavior, (b) seems to make that behavior re-occur more often in the future and (c) that

reoccurence of behavior must be the result of the change.

Nucleus accumbens	A complex of neurons that is part of the brain's "pleasure pathway" responsible for the experience of reward is referred to as the nucleus accumbens.
Pleasure center	Olds and Milner discovered that electrical stimulation of a particular region in the Mesolimbic dopamine system was highly rewarding to rats; they believed they had discovered the pleasure center in the brain. It now appears that stimulation of many regions of the mesolimbic system can lead to rewarding effects--the key is that dopamine ultimately reaches neurons in the nucleus accumbens, a limbic system structure.
Nucleus	In neuroanatomy, a cluster of cell bodies of neurons within the central nervous system is a nucleus.
Bipolar disorder	Bipolar Disorder is a mood disorder typically characterized by fluctuations between manic and depressive states; and, more generally, atypical mood regulation and mood instability.
Behavioral inhibition system	The behavioral inhibition system is a circuit in the limbic system that responds to threat signals by inhibiting activity and causing anxiety.
Behavioral inhibition	Physiological probes of children with behavioral inhibition show significantly higher measures of activity in the sympathetic nervous system and hypothalamic-pituitary axis than in non-inhibited children. Kagan postulates that anxiety-prone children are born with a lower firing threshold in amygdala and hypothalamic neurons. His work provides a robust model for predicting temperamental forerunners of anxiety disorders.
Stroop	The stroop interference effect occurs when a printed color word interferes with a person's ability to name the color of ink in which the word is printed if the ink color is not the same as the color named by the word.
Attention deficit hyperactivity disorder	A learning disability marked by inattention, impulsiveness, a low tolerance for frustration, and a great deal of inappropriate activity is the attention deficit hyperactivity disorder.
Norepinephrine	Norepinephrine is released from the adrenal glands as a hormone into the blood, but it is also a neurotransmitter in the nervous system. As a stress hormone, it affects parts of the human brain where attention and impulsivity are controlled. Along with epinephrine, this compound effects the fight-or-flight response, activating the sympathetic nervous system to directly increase heart rate, release energy from fat, and increase muscle readiness.
Hyperactivity	Hyperactivity can be described as a state in which a individual is abnormally easily excitable and exuberant. Strong emotional reactions and a very short span of attention is also typical for the individual.
Assertiveness	Assertiveness basically means the ability to express your thoughts and feelings in a way that clearly states your needs and keeps the lines of communication open with the other.
Homogeneous	In biology homogeneous has a meaning similar to its meaning in mathematics. Generally it means "the same" or "of the same quality or general property".
Feedback	Feedback refers to information returned to a person about the effects a response has had.
Goal-directed behavior	Goal-directed behavior is means-end problem solving behavior. In the infant, such behavior is first observed in the latter part of the first year.
Projection	Attributing one's own undesirable thoughts, impulses, traits, or behaviors to others is referred to as projection.
Incentive	An incentive is what is expected once a behavior is performed. An incentive acts as a

Go to **Cram101.com** for the Practice Tests for this Chapter.

	reinforcer.
Personality trait	According to the Diagnostic and Statistical Manual of the American Psychiatric Association, a personality trait is a "prominent aspect of personality that is exhibited in a wide range of important social and personal contexts. ...".
Substance abuse	Substance abuse refers to the overindulgence in and dependence on a stimulant, depressant, or other chemical substance, leading to effects that are detrimental to the individual's physical or mental health, or the welfare of others.
Double-blind	In a double-blind experiment, neither the individuals nor the researchers know who belongs to the control group. Only after all the data are recorded may researchers be permitted to learn which individuals are which. Performing an experiment in double-blind fashion is a way to lessen the influence of prejudices and unintentional physical cues on the results.
Amphetamine	Amphetamine is a synthetic stimulant used to suppress the appetite, control weight, and treat disorders including narcolepsy and ADHD. It is also used recreationally and for performance enhancement.
Placebo	Placebo refers to a bogus treatment that has the appearance of being genuine.
Biological predisposition	The genetic readiness of animals and humans to perform certain behaviors is a biological predisposition.
Social learning	Social learning is learning that occurs as a function of observing, retaining and replicating behavior observed in others. Although social learning can occur at any stage in life, it is thought to be particularly important during childhood, particularly as authority becomes important.
Habit	A habit is a response that has become completely separated from its eliciting stimulus. Early learning theorists used the term to describe S-R associations, however not all S-R associations become a habit, rather many are extinguished after reinforcement is withdrawn.
Alcoholic	An alcoholic is dependent on alcohol as characterized by craving, loss of control, physical dependence and withdrawal symptoms, and tolerance.
Behavioral genetics	Behavioral genetics is the field of biology that studies the role of genetics in behavior.
Neuroscience	A field that combines the work of psychologists, biologists, biochemists, medical researchers, and others in the study of the structure and function of the nervous system is neuroscience.
Genetics	Genetics is the science of genes, heredity, and the variation of organisms.
Analogy	An analogy is a comparison between two different things, in order to highlight some form of similarity. Analogy is the cognitive process of transferring information from a particular subject to another particular subject.
Positive relationship	Statistically, a positive relationship refers to a mathematical relationship in which increases in one measure are matched by increases in the other.
Self-esteem	Self-esteem refers to a person's subjective appraisal of himself or herself as intrinsically positive or negative to some degree.
Reductionism	Reductionism holds that the nature of complex things can always be reduced to (be explained by) simpler or more fundamental things.
Cognition	The intellectual processes through which information is obtained, transformed, stored, retrieved, and otherwise used is cognition.
Biological model	An explanation of a psychological dysfunction that primarily emphasizes brain disorder or

Go to **Cram101.com** for the Practice Tests for this Chapter.
And, **NEVER** highlight a book again!

illness as the cause is called a biological model.

Behaviorism	The school of psychology that defines psychology as the study of observable behavior and studies relationships between stimuli and responses is called behaviorism. Behaviorism relied heavily on animal research and stated the same principles governed the behavior of both nonhumans and humans.
Radical behaviorism	Skinner defined behavior to include everything that an organism does, including thinking, feeling and speaking and argued that these phenomena were valid subject matters of psychology. The term Radical Behaviorism refers to "everything an organism does is a behavior."
Psychoanalytic	Freud's theory that unconscious forces act as determinants of personality is called psychoanalytic theory. The theory is a developmental theory characterized by critical stages of development.
Titchener	Titchener attempted to classify the structures of the mind, not unlike the way a chemist breaks down chemicals into their component parts-water into hydrogen and oxygen for example. He conceived of hydrogen and oxygen as structures of a chemical compound, and sensations and thoughts as structures of the mind. This approach became known as structuralism.
Personality	Personality refers to the pattern of enduring characteristics that differentiates a person, the patterns of behaviors that make each individual unique.
Learning	Learning is a relatively permanent change in behavior that results from experience. Thus, to attribute a behavioral change to learning, the change must be relatively permanent and must result from experience.
Habit	A habit is a response that has become completely separated from its eliciting stimulus. Early learning theorists used the term to describe S-R associations, however not all S-R associations become a habit, rather many are extinguished after reinforcement is withdrawn.
Psychological test	Psychological test refers to a standardized measure of a sample of a person's behavior.
Emotion	An emotion is a mental states that arise spontaneously, rather than through conscious effort. They are often accompanied by physiological changes.
Reinforcement	In operant conditioning, reinforcement is any change in an environment that (a) occurs after the behavior, (b) seems to make that behavior re-occur more often in the future and (c) that reoccurence of behavior must be the result of the change.
Idiographic	An idiographic investigation studies the characteristics of an individual in depth.
Individual differences	Individual differences psychology studies the ways in which individual people differ in their behavior. This is distinguished from other aspects of psychology in that although psychology is ostensibly a study of individuals, modern psychologists invariably study groups.
Personality trait	According to the Diagnostic and Statistical Manual of the American Psychiatric Association, a personality trait is a "prominent aspect of personality that is exhibited in a wide range of important social and personal contexts. ...".
Trait	An enduring personality characteristic that tends to lead to certain behaviors is called a trait. The term trait also means a genetically inherited feature of an organism.
John Watson	John Watson, the father of behaviorism, developed the term "Behaviorism" as a name for his proposal to revolutionize the study of human psychology in order to put it on a firm experimental footing.
Skinner	Skinner conducted research on shaping behavior through positive and negative reinforcement, and demonstrated operant conditioning, a technique which he developed in contrast with classical conditioning.

Inclusiveness	Inclusiveness is a principle of organization in which a larger percieved configuration hides smaller ones.
Motivation	In psychology, motivation is the driving force (desire) behind all actions of an organism.
Early adulthood	The developmental period beginning in the late teens or early twenties and lasting into the thirties is called early adulthood; characterized by an increasing self-awareness.
Friendship	The essentials of friendship are reciprocity and commitment between individuals who see themselves more or less as equals. Interaction between friends rests on a more equal power base than the interaction between children and adults.
Anxiety	Anxiety is a complex combination of the feeling of fear, apprehension and worry often accompanied by physical sensations such as palpitations, chest pain and/or shortness of breath.
Neurosis	Neurosis, any mental disorder that, although may cause distress, does not interfere with rational thought or the persons' ability to function.
Theories	Theories are logically self-consistent models or frameworks describing the behavior of a certain natural or social phenomenon. They are broad explanations and predictions concerning phenomena of interest.
Modeling	A type of behavior learned through observation of others demonstrating the same behavior is modeling.
Archetype	The archetype is a concept of psychologist Carl Jung. They are innate prototypes for ideas, which may subsequently become involved in the interpretation of observed phenomena. A group of memories and interpretations closely associated with an archetype is called a complex.
Attention	Attention is the cognitive process of selectively concentrating on one thing while ignoring other things. Psychologists have labeled three types of attention: sustained attention, selective attention, and divided attention.
Jung	Jung was in some aspects a response to Sigmund Freud's psychoanalysis. He proposed and developed the concepts of the extroverted and introverted personality, archetypes, and the collective unconscious. His work has been influential in psychiatry and in the study of religion, literature, and related fields.
Psychodynamic	Most psychodynamic approaches are centered around the idea of a maladapted function developed early in life (usually childhood) which are at least in part unconscious. This maladapted function (a.k.a. defense mechanism) does not do well in place of a normal/healthy one.
Generativity	Generativity refers to an adult's concern for and commitment to the well-being of future generations.
Ethnic identity	An enduring, basic aspect of the self that includes a sense of membership in an ethnic group and the attitudes and feelings related to that membership is called an ethnic identity.
Role model	A person who serves as a positive example of desirable behavior is referred to as a role model.
Adolescence	The period of life bounded by puberty and the assumption of adult responsibilities is adolescence.
Social learning theory	Social learning theory explains the process of gender typing in terms of observation, imitation, and role playing .
Social learning	Social learning is learning that occurs as a function of observing, retaining and replicating behavior observed in others. Although social learning can occur at any stage in life, it is thought to be particularly important during childhood, particularly as authority becomes

important.

Mischel	Mischel is known for his cognitive social learning model of personality that focuses on the specific cognitive variables that mediate the manner in which new experiences affect the individual.
Society	The social sciences use the term society to mean a group of people that form a semi-closed (or semi-open) social system, in which most interactions are with other individuals belonging to the group.
Diphtheria	Diphtheria is an upper respiratory tract illness characterized by sore throat, low-grade fever, and an adherent membrane of the tonsil(s), pharynx, and/or nose.
Alcoholism	A disorder that involves long-term, repeated, uncontrolled, compulsive, and excessive use of alcoholic beverages and that impairs the drinker's health and work and social relationships is called alcoholism.
Rape	Rape is a crime where the victim is forced into sexual activity, in particular sexual penetration, against his or her will.
Social skills	Social skills are skills used to interact and communicate with others to assist status in the social structure and other motivations.
Punishment	Punishment is the addtion of a stimulus that reduces the frequency of a response, or the removal of a stimulus that results in a reduction of the response.
Functional analysis	A systematic study of behavior in which one identifies the stimuli that trigger the behavior and the reinforcers that maintain it is a functional analysis. Relations between the two become the cause-and-effect relationships in behavior and are the laws of a science. A synthesis of these various laws expressed in quantitative terms yields a comprehensive picture of the organism as a behaving system without postulating internal processes.
Reinforcer	In operant conditioning, a reinforcer is any stimulus that increases the probability that a preceding behavior will occur again. In Classical Conditioning, the unconditioned stimulus (US) is the reinforcer.
Adaptation	Adaptation is a lowering of sensitivity to a stimulus following prolonged exposure to that stimulus. Behavioral adaptations are special ways a particular organism behaves to survive in its natural habitat.
Adler	Adler argued that human personality could be explained teleologically, separate strands dominated by the guiding purpose of the individual's unconscious self ideal to convert feelings of inferiority to superiority (or rather completeness). The desires of the self ideal were countered by social and ethical demands.
Autonomy	Autonomy is the condition of something that does not depend on anything else.
Stages	Stages represent relatively discrete periods of time in which functioning is qualitatively different from functioning at other periods.
Humanistic	Humanistic refers to any system of thought focused on subjective experience and human problems and potentials.
Alcoholic	An alcoholic is dependent on alcohol as characterized by craving, loss of control, physical dependence and withdrawal symptoms, and tolerance.
Maslow	Maslow is mostly noted today for his proposal of a hierarchy of human needs which he often presented as a pyramid. Maslow was an instrumental player in the formation of the humanistic movement, also known as the third force in psychology.
Feedback	Feedback refers to information returned to a person about the effects a response has had.

Stroke	A stroke occurs when the blood supply to a part of the brain is suddenly interrupted by occlusion, by hemorrhage, or other causes
Achievement motivation	The psychological need in humans for success is called achievement motivation.
Punisher	Punisher refers to any event that decreases the probability or frequency of the response it follows.
Biological predisposition	The genetic readiness of animals and humans to perform certain behaviors is a biological predisposition.
Predisposition	Predisposition refers to an inclination or diathesis to respond in a certain way, either inborn or acquired. In abnormal psychology, it is a factor that lowers the ability to withstand stress and inclines the individual toward pathology.
Behavior modification	Behavior Modification is a technique of altering an individual's reactions to stimuli through positive reinforcement and the extinction of maladaptive behavior.
Stimulus control	Linking a particular response with specific stimuli is called stimulus control.
Stimulus	A change in an environmental condition that elicits a response is a stimulus.
Child development	Scientific study of the processes of change from conception through adolescence is called child development.
Animal model	An animal model usually refers to a non-human animal with a disease that is similar to a human condition.
Cognition	The intellectual processes through which information is obtained, transformed, stored, retrieved, and otherwise used is cognition.
Acute	Acute means sudden, sharp, and abrupt. Usually short in duration.
Physiology	The study of the functions and activities of living cells, tissues, and organs and of the physical and chemical phenomena involved is referred to as physiology.
Allport	Allport was a trait theorist. Those traits he believed to predominate a person's personality were called central traits. Traits such that one could be indentifed by the trait, were referred to as cardinal traits. Central traits and cardinal traits are influenced by environmental factors.
Conditioning	Conditioning describes the process by which behaviors can be learned or modified through interaction with the environment.
Depression	In everyday language depression refers to any downturn in mood, which may be relatively transitory and perhaps due to something trivial. This is differentiated from Clinical depression which is marked by symptoms that last two weeks or more and are so severe that they interfere with daily living.
Pavlov	Pavlov first described the phenomenon now known as classical conditioning in experiments with dogs.
Walden Two	Walden Two, a novel by B.F. Skinner, describes a fictional community designed around behavioral principles. The fictional utopian commune thrives on a level of productivity and happiness of its citizens far in advance of that in the outside world due to it's practice of scientific social planning and the use of operant conditioning in the raising of children.
Direct observation	Direct observation refers to assessing behavior through direct surveillance.
Empirical	Empirical means the use of working hypotheses which are capable of being disproved using

	observation or experiment.
Instinct	Instinct is the word used to describe inherent dispositions towards particular actions. They are generally an inherited pattern of responses or reactions to certain kinds of situations.
Natural selection	Natural selection is a process by which biological populations are altered over time, as a result of the propagation of heritable traits that affect the capacity of individual organisms to survive and reproduce.
Evolution	Commonly used to refer to gradual change, evolution is the change in the frequency of alleles within a population from one generation to the next. This change may be caused by different mechanisms, including natural selection, genetic drift, or changes in population (gene flow).
Adaptive behavior	An adaptive behavior increases the probability of the individual or organism to survive or exist within its environment.
Operant Conditioning	A simple form of learning in which an organism learns to engage in behavior because it is reinforced is referred to as operant conditioning. The consequences of a behavior produce changes in the probability of the behavior's occurence.
Thorndike	Thorndike worked in animal behavior and the learning process leading to the theory of connectionism. Among his most famous contributions were his research on cats escaping from puzzle boxes, and his formulation of the Law of Effect.
Operant behavior	Operant behavior is simply emitted by an organism, that is, all organisms are inherently active, emitting responses that operate in the environment. Unlike respondent behavior, which is dependent on the stimulus that preceded it, operant behavior is a function of its consequences.
Extinction	In operant extinction, if no reinforcement is delivered after the response, gradually the behavior will no longer occur in the presence of the stimulus. The process is more rapid following continuous reinforcement rather than after partial reinforcement. In Classical Conditioning, repeated presentations of the CS without being followed by the US results in the extinction of the CS.
Positive reinforcer	In operant conditioning, a stimulus that is presented after a response that increases the likelihood that the response will be repeated is a positive reinforcer.
Primary Reinforcer	Any stimulus whose reinforcing effect is immediate and not a function of previous experience is a primary reinforcer (eg, food, water, warmth).
Innate	Innate behavior is not learned or influenced by the environment, rather, it is present or predisposed at birth.
Negative reinforcement	During negative reinforcement, a stimulus is removed and the frequency of the behavior or response increases.
Negative reinforcer	Negative reinforcer is a reinforcer that when removed increases the frequency of an response.
Metaphor	A metaphor is a rhetorical trope where a comparison is made between two seemingly unrelated subjects
Aversive stimulus	A stimulus that elicits pain, fear, or avoidance is an aversive stimulus.
Generalization	In conditioning, the tendency for a conditioned response to be evoked by stimuli that are similar to the stimulus to which the response was conditioned is a generalization. The greater the similarity among the stimuli, the greater the probability of generalization.
Discrimination	In Learning theory, discrimination refers the ability to distinguish between a conditioned

	stimulus and other stimuli. It can be brought about by extensive training or differential reinforcement. In social terms, it is the denial of privileges to a person or a group on the basis of prejudice.
Chaining	Chaining involves reinforcing individual responses occurring in a sequence to form a complex behavior. It is frequently used for training behavioral sequences that are beyond the current repetoire of the learner.
Shaping	The concept of reinforcing successive, increasingly accurate approximations to a target behavior is called shaping. The target behavior is broken down into a hierarchy of elemental steps, each step more sophisticated then the last. By successively reinforcing each of the the elemental steps, a form of differential reinforcement, until that step is learned while extinguishing the step below, the target behavior is gradually achieved.
Successive approximations	In operant conditioning, a series of behaviors that gradually become more similar to a target behavior are called successive approximations.
Variable	A variable refers to a measurable factor, characteristic, or attribute of an individual or a system.
Discriminative stimulus	In operant conditioning, a stimulus that indicates that reinforcement is available upon the apporpriate response, is called the discriminative stimulus.
Ego	In Freud's view the Ego serves to balance our primitive needs and our moral beliefs and taboos. Relying on experience, a healthy Ego provides the ability to adapt to reality and interact with the outside world.
Discrimination training	Teaching an organism to show a response in the presence of only one of a series of similar stimuli is discrimination training. It is accomplished by alternating the stimuli and reinforcing only the target stimulus.
Stimulus discrimination	The tendency to make a response when stimuli previously associated with reinforcement are present and to withhold the response when not present, is stimulus discrimination.
Schedule of reinforcement	A schedule of reinforcement is either continuous (the behavior is reinforced each time it occurs) or intermittent (the behavior is reinforced only on certain occasions).
Continuous reinforcement	In continuous reinforcement, every response results in reinforcement.
Partial reinforcement	In a partial reinforcement environment, not every correct response is reinforced. Partial reinforcement is usually introduced after a continuous reinforcement schedule has acquired the behavior.
Resistance to extinction	Resistance to extinction is the phenomenon that occurs when an organism continues to make a response even after the delivery of the reinforcer for the response has been all or partially eliminated.
Variable ratio	In a variable ratio schedule of reinforcement, the number of responses required between reinforcements varies, but on average equals a predetermined number. The variable ratio schedule produces both the highest rate of responding and the greatest resistance to extinction.
Fixed interval	In a fixed interval schedule of reinforcement, reinforcement occurs after the passage of a specified length of time from the beginning of training or from the last reinforcement, provided that at least one response occurred in that time period.
Response rate	The response rate is usually calculated by dividing the total number of responses by the time available for the response.
Positive	In positive reinforcement, a stimulus is added and the rate of responding increases.

reinforcement	
Insight	Insight refers to a sudden awareness of the relationships among various elements that had previously appeared to be independent of one another.
Primary reinforcement	The use of reinforcers that are innately or biologically satisfying is called primary reinforcement.
Token economies	Token economies is a technique used in behavioral therapy where subjects are given a token (that can be traded for something desirable) as a form of positive reinforcement for appropriate behavior.
Population	Population refers to all members of a well-defined group of organisms, events, or things.
Social skills training	Social skills training refers to a behavior therapy designed to improve interpersonal skills that emphasizes shaping, modeling, and behavioral rehearsal.
Token economy	An environmental setting that fosters desired behavior by reinforcing it with tokens that can be exchanged for other reinforcers is called a token economy.
Creativity	Creativity is the ability to think about something in novel and unusual ways and come up with unique solutions to problems. It involves divergent thinking, having many solutions or views to a problem.
Developmentally disabled	developmentally disabled is a term for a pattern of persistently slow learning of basic motor and language skills during childhood, and a significantly below-normal global intellectual capacity as an adult.
Psychotherapy	Psychotherapy is a set of techniques based on psychological principles intended to improve mental health, emotional or behavioral issues.
Behavioral therapy	The treatment of a mental disorder through the application of basic principles of conditioning and learning is called behavioral therapy.
Psychoanalysis	Psychoanalysis refers to the school of psychology that emphasizes the importance of unconscious motives and conflicts as determinants of human behavior. It was Freud's method of exploring human personality.
Programmed instruction	Programmed instruction is characterized by clearly stated behavioral objectives, small frames of instruction, self-pacing, active learner response to inserted questions, and immediate feedback regarding the correctness of a response.
Carl Rogers	Carl Rogers was instrumental in the development of non-directive psychotherapy, also known as "client-centered" psychotherapy. Rogers' basic tenets were unconditional positive regard, genuineness, and empathic understanding, with each demonstrated by the counselor.
Utopian	An ideal vision of society is a utopian society.
Verbal Behavior	Verbal Behavior is a book written by B.F. Skinner in which the author presents his ideas on language. For Skinner, speech, along with other forms of communication, was simply a behavior. Skinner argued that each act of speech is an inevitable consequence of the speaker's current environment and his behavioral and sensory history.
Chomsky	Chomsky has greatly influenced the field of theoretical linguistics with his work on the theory of generative grammar. Accordingly, humans are biologically prewired to learn language at a certain time and in a certain way.
Personality psychology	Personality psychology is a branch of psychology which studies personality and individual difference processes. One emphasis in personality psychology is on trying to create a coherent picture of a person and all his or her major psychological processes.
Overt behavior	An action or response that is directly observable and measurable is an overt behavior.

Go to **Cram101.com** for the Practice Tests for this Chapter.

Neuroscience	A field that combines the work of psychologists, biologists, biochemists, medical researchers, and others in the study of the structure and function of the nervous system is neuroscience.
Classical conditioning	Classical conditioning is a simple form of learning in which an organism comes to associate or anticipate events. A neutral stimulus comes to evoke the response usually evoked by a natural or unconditioned stimulus by being paired repeatedly with the unconditioned stimulus.
Standardized test	An oral or written assessment for which an individual receives a score indicating how the individual reponded relative to a previously tested large sample of others is referred to as a standardized test.
Positivism	Positivism is an approach to understanding the world based on science. It can be traced back to Auguste Comte in the 19th century. Positivists believe that there is little if any methodological difference between social sciences and natural sciences; societies, like nature, operate according to laws.
Paradigm	Paradigm refers to the set of practices that defines a scientific discipline during a particular period of time. It provides a framework from which to conduct research, it ensures that a certain range of phenomena, those on which the paradigm focuses, are explored thoroughly. Itmay also blind scientists to other, perhaps more fruitful, ways of dealing with their subject matter.
American Psychological Association	The American Psychological Association is a professional organization representing psychology in the US. The mission statement is to "advance psychology as a science and profession and as a means of promoting health, education , and human welfare".
Time-out	Time-out is an operant conditioning punishment procedure in which, after unwanted behavior, the person is temporarily removed from a setting--in theory, a removal of stimuli resulting in an increase in the frequency of wanted behaviors; an example of negative reinforcement.
Skinner box	An operant conditioning chamber, or Skinner box, is an experimental apparatus used to study conditioning in animals. Chambers have at least one operandum that can automatically detect the occurrence of a behavioral response or action. The other minimal requirement of a conditioning chamber is that it have a means of delivering a primary reinforcer or unconditioned stimulus like food or water.
Incentive	An incentive is what is expected once a behavior is performed. An incentive acts as a reinforcer.
Intelligence test	An intelligence test is a standardized means of assessing a person's current mental ability, for example, the Stanford-Binet test and the Wechsler Adult Intelligence Scale.
Maladaptive	In psychology, a behavior or trait is adaptive when it helps an individual adjust and function well within their social environment. A maladaptive behavior or trait is counterproductive to the individual.
Personality test	A personality test aims to describe aspects of a person's character that remain stable across situations.
Early childhood	Early childhood refers to the developmental period extending from the end of infancy to about 5 or 6 years of age; sometimes called the preschool years.
Attitude	An enduring mental representation of a person, place, or thing that evokes an emotional response and related behavior is called attitude.
Affect	A subjective feeling or emotional tone often accompanied by bodily expressions noticeable to others is called affect.
Mental	Mental retardation refers to having significantly below-average intellectual functioning and

Go to **Cram101.com** for the Practice Tests for this Chapter.

retardation	limitations in at least two areas of adaptive functioning. Many categorize retardation as mild, moderate, severe, or profound.
Defense mechanism	A Defense mechanism is a set of unconscious ways to protect one's personality from unpleasant thoughts and realities which may otherwise cause anxiety. The notion is an integral part of the psychoanalytic theory.
Paranoid	The term paranoid is typically used in a general sense to signify any self-referential delusion, or more specifically, to signify a delusion involving the fear of persecution.
Delusion	A false belief, not generally shared by others, and that cannot be changed despite strong evidence to the contrary is a delusion.
Self-concept	Self-concept refers to domain-specific evaluations of the self where a domain may be academics, athletics, etc.
Psychoanalyst	A psychoanalyst is a specially trained therapist who attempts to treat the individual by uncovering and revealing to the individual otherwise subconscious factors that are contributing to some undesirable behavor.
Hallucination	A hallucination is a sensory perception experienced in the absence of an external stimulus, as distinct from an illusion, which is a misperception of an external stimulus. They may occur in any sensory modality - visual, auditory, olfactory, gustatory, tactile, or mixed.
Psychological disorder	Mental processes and/or behavior patterns that cause emotional distress and/or substantial impairment in functioning is a psychological disorder.
Behavioral assessment	Direct measures of an individual's behavior used to describe characteristics indicative of personality are called behavioral assessment.
Community psychology	Community psychology is the study of how to use the principles of psychology to create communities of all sizes that promote mental health of their members.
Nature-nurture	Nature-nurture is a shorthand expression for debates about the relative importance of an individual's "nature" versus personal experiences ("nurture") in determining or causing physical and behavioral traits.
Trauma	Trauma refers to a severe physical injury or wound to the body caused by an external force, or a psychological shock having a lasting effect on mental life.
Down syndrome	Down syndrome encompasses a number of genetic disorders, of which trisomy 21 (a nondisjunction, the so-called extrachromosone) is the most representative, causing highly variable degrees of learning difficulties as well as physical disabilities. Incidence of Down syndrome is estimated at 1 per 660 births, making it the most common chromosomal abnormality.
Syndrome	The term syndrome is the association of several clinically recognizable features, signs, symptoms, phenomena or characteristics which often occur together, so that the presence of one feature indicates the presence of the others.
Heredity	Heredity is the transfer of characteristics from parent to offspring through their genes.
Cooing	Cooing is the spontaneous repetition of vowel sounds by infants.
Questionnaire	A self-report method of data collection or clinical assessment method in which the individual being studied checks off items on a printed list, answers multiple-choice questions, or writes out answers to essay questions aimed at producing a selfdescription is called questionnaire.
Agreeableness	Agreeableness, one of the big-five personality traits, reflects individual differences in concern with cooperation and social harmony. It is the degree individuals value getting along with others.

Laboratory setting	Research setting in which the behavior of interest does not naturally occur is called a laboratory setting.
Self-report method	The self-report method is an experimental design in which the people being studied are asked to rate or describe their own behaviors or mental states.
Operational definition	An operational definition is the definition of a concept or action in terms of the observable and repeatable process, procedures, and appartaus that illustrates the concept or action.
Acquisition	Acquisition is the process of adapting to the environment, learning or becoming conditioned. In classical conditoning terms, it is the initial learning of the stimulus response link, which involves a neutral stimulus being associated with a unconditioned stimulus and becoming a conditioned stimulus.
Schedules of Reinforcement	Different combinations of frequency and timing of reinforcement following a behavior are referred to as schedules of reinforcement. They are either continuous (the behavior is reinforced each time it occurs) or intermittent (the behavior is reinforced only on certain occasions).
Ratio schedules	Ratio schedules produce higher rates of responding than interval schedules.
Species	Species refers to a reproductively isolated breeding population.
Pathology	Pathology is the study of the processes underlying disease and other forms of illness, harmful abnormality, or dysfunction.

Learning	Learning is a relatively permanent change in behavior that results from experience. Thus, to attribute a behavioral change to learning, the change must be relatively permanent and must result from experience.
Insight	Insight refers to a sudden awareness of the relationships among various elements that had previously appeared to be independent of one another.
Punishment	Punishment is the addtion of a stimulus that reduces the frequency of a response, or the removal of a stimulus that results in a reduction of the response.
Personality	Personality refers to the pattern of enduring characteristics that differentiates a person, the patterns of behaviors that make each individual unique.
Psychoanalyst	A psychoanalyst is a specially trained therapist who attempts to treat the individual by uncovering and revealing to the individual otherwise subconscious factors that are contributing to some undesirable behavor.
Adaptation	Adaptation is a lowering of sensitivity to a stimulus following prolonged exposure to that stimulus. Behavioral adaptations are special ways a particular organism behaves to survive in its natural habitat.
Ego	In Freud's view the Ego serves to balance our primitive needs and our moral beliefs and taboos. Relying on experience, a healthy Ego provides the ability to adapt to reality and interact with the outside world.
Alcoholism	A disorder that involves long-term, repeated, uncontrolled, compulsive, and excessive use of alcoholic beverages and that impairs the drinker's health and work and social relationships is called alcoholism.
Rape	Rape is a crime where the victim is forced into sexual activity, in particular sexual penetration, against his or her will.
Learned helplessness	Learned helplessness is a description of the effect of inescapable positive punishment (such as electrical shock) on animal (and by extension, human) behavior.
Neurosis	Neurosis, any mental disorder that, although may cause distress, does not interfere with rational thought or the persons' ability to function.
Syndrome	The term syndrome is the association of several clinically recognizable features, signs, symptoms, phenomena or characteristics which often occur together, so that the presence of one feature indicates the presence of the others.
Suppression	Suppression is the defense mechanism where a memory is deliberately forgotten.
Incentive	An incentive is what is expected once a behavior is performed. An incentive acts as a reinforcer.
Defense mechanism	A Defense mechanism is a set of unconscious ways to protect one's personality from unpleasant thoughts and realities which may otherwise cause anxiety. The notion is an integral part of the psychoanalytic theory.
Displacement	An unconscious defense mechanism in which the individual directs aggressive or sexual feelings away from the primary object to someone or something safe is referred to as displacement. Displacement in linguistics is simply the ability to talk about things not present.
Stimulus	A change in an environmental condition that elicits a response is a stimulus.
Theories	Theories are logically self-consistent models or frameworks describing the behavior of a certain natural or social phenomenon. They are broad explanations and predictions concerning phenomena of interest.

Go to **Cram101.com** for the Practice Tests for this Chapter.

Society	The social sciences use the term society to mean a group of people that form a semi-closed (or semi-open) social system, in which most interactions are with other individuals belonging to the group.
Discrimination	In Learning theory, discrimination refers the ability to distinguish between a conditioned stimulus and other stimuli. It can be brought about by extensive training or differential reinforcement. In social terms, it is the denial of privileges to a person or a group on the basis of prejudice.
Motivation	In psychology, motivation is the driving force (desire) behind all actions of an organism.
Child development	Scientific study of the processes of change from conception through adolescence is called child development.
Stages	Stages represent relatively discrete periods of time in which functioning is qualitatively different from functioning at other periods.
Psychoanalytic theory	Psychoanalytic theory is a general term for approaches to psychoanalysis which attempt to provide a conceptual framework more-or-less independent of clinical practice rather than based on empirical analysis of clinical cases.
Psychoanalytic	Freud's theory that unconscious forces act as determinants of personality is called psychoanalytic theory. The theory is a developmental theory characterized by critical stages of development.
Psychoanalysis	Psychoanalysis refers to the school of psychology that emphasizes the importance of unconscious motives and conflicts as determinants of human behavior. It was Freud's method of exploring human personality.
Neal Miller	Neal Miller introduced the concepts of the approach gradient and avoidance gradient. Whether organisms drive toward or away from a positive stimulus or a negative stimulus is a function of the distance that it is from that stimulus.
Social class	Social class describes the relationships between people in hierarchical societies or cultures. Those with more power usually subordinate those with less power.
Variable	A variable refers to a measurable factor, characteristic, or attribute of an individual or a system.
Laboratory setting	Research setting in which the behavior of interest does not naturally occur is called a laboratory setting.
Psychotherapy	Psychotherapy is a set of techniques based on psychological principles intended to improve mental health, emotional or behavioral issues.
Physiological psychology	Physiological psychology refers to the study of the physiological mechanisms, in the brain and elsewhere, that mediate behavior and psychological experiences.
Basic research	Basic research has as its primary objective the advancement of knowledge and the theoretical understanding of the relations among variables . It is exploratory and often driven by the researcher's curiosity, interest or hunch.
Anxiety	Anxiety is a complex combination of the feeling of fear, apprehension and worry often accompanied by physical sensations such as palpitations, chest pain and/or shortness of breath.
American Psychological Association	The American Psychological Association is a professional organization representing psychology in the US. The mission statement is to "advance psychology as a science and profession and as a means of promoting health, education , and human welfare".
Autonomic	A division of the peripheral nervous system, the autonomic nervous system, regulates glands

Go to **Cram101.com** for the Practice Tests for this Chapter.

nervous system	and activities such as heartbeat, respiration, digestion, and dilation of the pupils. It is responsible for homeostasis, maintaining a relatively constant internal environment .
Nervous system	The body's electrochemical communication circuitry, made up of billions of neurons is a nervous system.
Biofeedback	Biofeedback is the process of measuring and quantifying an aspect of a subject's physiology, analyzing the data, and then feeding back the information to the subject in a form that allows the subject to enact physiological change.
Scientific method	Psychologists gather data in order to describe, understand, predict, and control behavior. Scientific method refers to an approach that can be used to discover accurate information. It includes these steps: understand the problem, collect data, draw conclusions, and revise research conclusions.
Social learning	Social learning is learning that occurs as a function of observing, retaining and replicating behavior observed in others. Although social learning can occur at any stage in life, it is thought to be particularly important during childhood, particularly as authority becomes important.
Psychopathology	Psychopathology refers to the field concerned with the nature and development of mental disorders.
Animal model	An animal model usually refers to a non-human animal with a disease that is similar to a human condition.
Thorndike	Thorndike worked in animal behavior and the learning process leading to the theory of connectionism. Among his most famous contributions were his research on cats escaping from puzzle boxes, and his formulation of the Law of Effect.
Skinner	Skinner conducted research on shaping behavior through positive and negative reinforcement, and demonstrated operant conditioning, a technique which he developed in contrast with classical conditioning.
Pavlov	Pavlov first described the phenomenon now known as classical conditioning in experiments with dogs.
Hull	Hull is best known for the Drive Reduction Theory which postulated that behavior occurs in response to primary drives such as hunger, thirst, sexual interest, etc. When the goal of the drive is attained the drive is reduced. This reduction of drive serves as a reinforcer for learning.
Generalization	In conditioning, the tendency for a conditioned response to be evoked by stimuli that are similar to the stimulus to which the response was conditioned is a generalization. The greater the similarity among the stimuli, the greater the probability of generalization.
Conditioning	Conditioning describes the process by which behaviors can be learned or modified through interaction with the environment.
Extinction	In operant extinction, if no reinforcement is delivered after the response, gradually the behavior will no longer occur in the presence of the stimulus. The process is more rapid following continuous reinforcement rather than after partial reinforcement. In Classical Conditioning, repeated presentations of the CS without being followed by the US results in the extinction of the CS.
Miller and Dollard	Miller and Dollard extended Hull's theory into human social learning conditions. The Social Learning Theory was officially launched in 1941 with their publication of Social Learning and Imitation. It incorporated the principles of Hullian learning: reinforcement, punishment, extinction, and imitation of models.

Libido	Sigmund Freud suggested that libido is the instinctual energy or force that can come into conflict with the conventions of civilized behavior. Jung, condidered the libido as the free creative, or psychic, energy an individual has to put toward personal development, or individuation.
Primary drive	A primary drive is a state of tension or arousal arising from a biological or innate need; it is one not based on learning. A primary drive activates behavior.
Response hierarchy	The ordering of a series of responses according to the likelihood of their being elicited by a particular stimulus is called a response hierarchy.
Drive reduction	Drive reduction theories are based on the need-state. Drive activates behavior. Reinforcement occurs whenever drive is reduced, leading to learning of whatever response solves the need. Thus the reduction in need serves as reinforcement and produces reinforcement of the response that leads to it.
A priori	The term A Priori is considered to mean propositional knowledge that can be had without, or "prior to", experience.
Innate	Innate behavior is not learned or influenced by the environment, rather, it is present or predisposed at birth.
Overt behavior	An action or response that is directly observable and measurable is an overt behavior.
Spontaneous recovery	The recurrence of an extinguished response as a function of the passage of time is referred to as spontaneous recovery.
Stimulus generalization	When animals are trained to respond to a single stimulus and test stimuli are introduced that differ from the training stimulus, generally along a single dimension, the systematic decrement in responding typically found has been called the gradient of stimulus generalization.
Obedience	Obedience is the willingness to follow the will of others. Humans have been shown to be surprisingly obedient in the presence of perceived legitimate authority figures, as demonstrated by the Milgram experiment in the 1960s.
Reinforcement	In operant conditioning, reinforcement is any change in an environment that (a) occurs after the behavior, (b) seems to make that behavior re-occur more often in the future and (c) that reoccurence of behavior must be the result of the change.
Conformity	Conformity is the degree to which members of a group will change their behavior, views and attitudes to fit the views of the group. The group can influence members via unconscious processes or via overt social pressure on individuals.
Trait	An enduring personality characteristic that tends to lead to certain behaviors is called a trait. The term trait also means a genetically inherited feature of an organism.
Anal stage	The anal stage in psychology is the term used by Sigmund Freud to describe the development during the second year of life, in which a child's pleasure and conflict centers are in the anal area.
Superego	Frued's third psychic structure, which functions as a moral guardian and sets forth high standards for behavior is the superego.
Guilt	Guilt describes many concepts related to a negative emotion or condition caused by actions which are believed to be, morally wrong. According to Freud, the avoidance of guilt is the basis for moral behavior.
Masturbation	Masturbation is the manual excitation of the sexual organs, most often to the point of orgasm. It can refer to excitation either by oneself or by another, but commonly refers to such activities performed alone.

171

Phobia	A persistent, irrational fear of an object, situation, or activity that the person feels compelled to avoid is referred to as a phobia.
Castration	Castration is any action, surgical, chemical or otherwise, by which a biological male loses use of the testes. This causes sterilization, i.e. prevents him from reproducing; it also greatly reduces the production of certain hormones, such as testosterone.
Attitude	An enduring mental representation of a person, place, or thing that evokes an emotional response and related behavior is called attitude.
Repression	A defense mechanism, repression involves moving thoughts unacceptable to the ego into the unconscious, where they cannot be easily accessed.
Intrapsychic conflict	In psychoanalysis, the struggles among the id, ego, and superego are an intrapsychic conflict.
Approach-avoidance conflict	Approach-avoidance conflict refers to the tension experienced by people when they are simultaneously attracted to and repulsed by the same goal.
Avoidance-avoidance conflict	A type of conflict in which the goals are negative, but avoidance of one requires approaching the other is an avoidance-avoidance conflict.
Approach-approach conflict	A type of conflict in which the goals that produce opposing motives are positive and within reach is referred to as an approach-approach conflict.
Double approach-avoidance conflict	Double approach-avoidance conflict refers to being simultaneously attracted to and repelled by each of two alternatives.
Death instinct	The death instinct was defined by Sigmund Freud, in Beyond the Pleasure Principle(1920). It speculated on the existence of a fundamental death wish or death instinct, referring to an individual's own need to die.
Instinct	Instinct is the word used to describe inherent dispositions towards particular actions. They are generally an inherited pattern of responses or reactions to certain kinds of situations.
Sears	Sears focused on the application of the social learning theory (SLT) to socialization processes, and how children internalize the values, attitudes, and behaviors predominant in their culture. He articulated the place of parents in fostering internalization. In addition, he was among the first social learning theorists to officially acknowledge the reciprocal interaction on an individual's behavior and their environment
Hypothesis	A specific statement about behavior or mental processes that is testable through research is a hypothesis.
Authoritarian	The term authoritarian is used to describe a style that enforces strong and sometimes oppressive measures against those in its sphere of influence, generally without attempts at gaining their consent.
Deprivation	Deprivation, is the loss or withholding of normal stimulation, nutrition, comfort, love, and so forth; a condition of lacking. The level of stimulation is less than what is required.
Prejudice	Prejudice in general, implies coming to a judgment on the subject before learning where the preponderance of the evidence actually lies, or formation of a judgement without direct experience.
Working hypothesis	A simple statement of what is expected to happen in an experiment is a working hypothesis.

Catharsis	Catharsis has been adopted by modern psychotherapy as the act of giving expression to deep emotions often associated with events in the individuals past which have never before been adequately expressed.
Displaced aggression	Redirecting aggression to a target other than the actual source of one's frustration is a defense mechanism called displaced aggression.
Clinician	A health professional authorized to provide services to people suffering from one or more pathologies is a clinician.
Emotion	An emotion is a mental states that arise spontaneously, rather than through conscious effort. They are often accompanied by physiological changes.
Questionnaire	A self-report method of data collection or clinical assessment method in which the individual being studied checks off items on a printed list, answers multiple-choice questions, or writes out answers to essay questions aimed at producing a selfdescription is called questionnaire.
McGregor	McGregor, whose 1960 book The Human Side of Enterprise had a profound influence on management practices, identified an approach of creating an environment within which employees are motivated, which he called theory X and theory Y.
Self-esteem	Self-esteem refers to a person's subjective appraisal of himself or herself as intrinsically positive or negative to some degree.
Masculinity	Masculinity is a culturally determined value reflecting the set of characteristics of maleness.
Attachment	Attachment is the tendency to seek closeness to another person and feel secure when that person is present.
Individual differences	Individual differences psychology studies the ways in which individual people differ in their behavior. This is distinguished from other aspects of psychology in that although psychology is ostensibly a study of individuals, modern psychologists invariably study groups.
Limbic system	The limbic system is a group of brain structures that are involved in various emotions such as aggression, fear, pleasure and also in the formation of memory. The limbic system affects the endocrine system and the autonomic nervous system. It consists of several subcortical structures located around the thalamus.
Brain	The brain controls and coordinates most movement, behavior and homeostatic body functions such as heartbeat, blood pressure, fluid balance and body temperature. Functions of the brain are responsible for cognition, emotion, memory, motor learning and other sorts of learning. The brain is primarily made up of two types of cells: glia and neurons.
Prenatal	Prenatal period refers to the time from conception to birth.
Primary process	The primary process in psychoanalytic theory, is one of the id's means of reducing tension by imagining what it desires.
Trial and error	Trial and error is an approach to problem solving in which one solution after another is tried in no particular order until an answer is found.
Reasoning	Reasoning is the act of using reason to derive a conclusion from certain premises. There are two main methods to reach a conclusion,deductive reasoning and inductive reasoning.
Problem solving	An attempt to find an appropriate way of attaining a goal when the goal is not readily available is called problem solving.
Maladaptive	In psychology, a behavior or trait is adaptive when it helps an individual adjust and function well within their social environment. A maladaptive behavior or trait is

counterproductive to the individual.

Mental processes	The thoughts, feelings, and motives that each of us experiences privately but that cannot be observed directly are called mental processes.
Alcoholic	An alcoholic is dependent on alcohol as characterized by craving, loss of control, physical dependence and withdrawal symptoms, and tolerance.
Relearning	Relearning refers to a measure of retention used in experiments on memory. Material is usually relearned more quickly than it is learned initially.
Free association	In psychoanalysis, the uncensored uttering of all thoughts that come to mind is called free association.
Consciousness	The awareness of the sensations, thoughts, and feelings being experienced at a given moment is called consciousness.
Attention	Attention is the cognitive process of selectively concentrating on one thing while ignoring other things. Psychologists have labeled three types of attention: sustained attention, selective attention, and divided attention.
Post-traumatic stress disorder	Post-traumatic stress disorder is a term for the psychological consequences of exposure to or confrontation with stressful experiences, which involve actual or threatened death, serious physical injury or a threat to physical integrity and which the person found highly traumatic.
Stress disorder	A significant emotional disturbance caused by stresses outside the range of normal human experience is referred to as stress disorder.
Immune system	The most important function of the human immune system occurs at the cellular level of the blood and tissues. The lymphatic and blood circulation systems are highways for specialized white blood cells. These cells include B cells, T cells, natural killer cells, and macrophages. All function with the primary objective of recognizing, attacking and destroying bacteria, viruses, cancer cells, and all substances seen as foreign.
Depression	In everyday language depression refers to any downturn in mood, which may be relatively transitory and perhaps due to something trivial. This is differentiated from Clinical depression which is marked by symptoms that last two weeks or more and are so severe that they interfere with daily living.
Sympathetic	The sympathetic nervous system activates what is often termed the "fight or flight response". It is an automatic regulation system, that is, one that operates without the intervention of conscious thought.
Social perception	A subfield of social psychology that studies the ways in which we form and modify impressions of others is social perception.
Perception	Perception is the process of acquiring, interpreting, selecting, and organizing sensory information.
Cognition	The intellectual processes through which information is obtained, transformed, stored, retrieved, and otherwise used is cognition.
Neuroscience	A field that combines the work of psychologists, biologists, biochemists, medical researchers, and others in the study of the structure and function of the nervous system is neuroscience.
Psychosexual stages	In Freudian theory each child passes through five psychosexual stages. During each stage, the id focuses on a distinct erogenous zone on the body. Suffering from trauma during any of the first three stages may result in fixation in that stage. Freud related the resolutions of the stages with adult personalities and personality disorders.

| **Species** | Species refers to a reproductively isolated breeding population. |

Social learning	Social learning is learning that occurs as a function of observing, retaining and replicating behavior observed in others. Although social learning can occur at any stage in life, it is thought to be particularly important during childhood, particularly as authority becomes important.
Learning	Learning is a relatively permanent change in behavior that results from experience. Thus, to attribute a behavioral change to learning, the change must be relatively permanent and must result from experience.
Overt behavior	An action or response that is directly observable and measurable is an overt behavior.
Personality	Personality refers to the pattern of enduring characteristics that differentiates a person, the patterns of behaviors that make each individual unique.
Attention	Attention is the cognitive process of selectively concentrating on one thing while ignoring other things. Psychologists have labeled three types of attention: sustained attention, selective attention, and divided attention.
Cognitive psychology	Cognitive psychology is the psychological science which studies the mental processes that are hypothesised to underlie behavior. This covers a broad range of research domains, examining questions about the workings of memory, attention, perception, knowledge representation, reasoning, creativity and problem solving.
Mental processes	The thoughts, feelings, and motives that each of us experiences privately but that cannot be observed directly are called mental processes.
Emotion	An emotion is a mental states that arise spontaneously, rather than through conscious effort. They are often accompanied by physiological changes.
Behaviorism	The school of psychology that defines psychology as the study of observable behavior and studies relationships between stimuli and responses is called behaviorism. Behaviorism relied heavily on animal research and stated the same principles governed the behavior of both nonhumans and humans.
Cognitive approach	A cognitive approach focuses on the mental processes involved in knowing: how we direct our attention, perceive, remember, think, and solve problems.
Research design	A research design tests a hypothesis. The basic typess are: descriptive, correlational, and experimental.
Research method	The scope of the research method is to produce some new knowledge. This, in principle, can take three main forms: Exploratory research; Constructive research; and Empirical research.
Idiographic	An idiographic investigation studies the characteristics of an individual in depth.
Nomothetic	Nomothetic measures are contrasted to ipsative or idiothetic measures, where nomothetic measures are measures that can be taken directly by an outside observer, such as weight or how many times a particular behavior occurs, and ipsative measures are self-reports such as a rank-ordered list of preferences.
Skinner	Skinner conducted research on shaping behavior through positive and negative reinforcement, and demonstrated operant conditioning, a technique which he developed in contrast with classical conditioning.
Meningitis	Meningitis is inflammation of the membranes covering the brain and the spinal cord. Although the most common causes are infection (bacterial, viral, fungal or parasitic), chemical agents and even tumor cells may cause meningitis.
Construct	A generalized concept, such as anxiety or gravity, is a construct.
Mischel	Mischel is known for his cognitive social learning model of personality that focuses on the

Go to **Cram101.com** for the Practice Tests for this Chapter.

	specific cognitive variables that mediate the manner in which new experiences affect the individual.
Trait	An enduring personality characteristic that tends to lead to certain behaviors is called a trait. The term trait also means a genetically inherited feature of an organism.
Ego	In Freud's view the Ego serves to balance our primitive needs and our moral beliefs and taboos. Relying on experience, a healthy Ego provides the ability to adapt to reality and interact with the outside world.
Reciprocal Determinism	Bandura's term for the social-cognitive view that people influence their environment just as their environment influences them is reciprocal determinism.
Determinism	Determinism is the philosophical proposition that every event, including human cognition and action, is causally determined by an unbroken chain of prior occurrences.
Bandura	Bandura is best known for his work on social learning theory or Social Cognitivism. His famous Bobo doll experiment illustrated that people learn from observing others.
Cognition	The intellectual processes through which information is obtained, transformed, stored, retrieved, and otherwise used is cognition.
Polarization	Polarization is the process of preparing a neuron for firing by creating an internal negative charge in relation to the body fluid outside the cell membrane.
Theories	Theories are logically self-consistent models or frameworks describing the behavior of a certain natural or social phenomenon. They are broad explanations and predictions concerning phenomena of interest.
Jung	Jung was in some aspects a response to Sigmund Freud's psychoanalysis. He proposed and developed the concepts of the extroverted and introverted personality, archetypes, and the collective unconscious. His work has been influential in psychiatry and in the study of religion, literature, and related fields.
Reinforcement	In operant conditioning, reinforcement is any change in an environment that (a) occurs after the behavior, (b) seems to make that behavior re-occur more often in the future and (c) that reoccurence of behavior must be the result of the change.
Displaced aggression	Redirecting aggression to a target other than the actual source of one's frustration is a defense mechanism called displaced aggression.
Self-actualization	Self-actualization (a term originated by Kurt Goldstein) is the instinctual need of a human to make the most of their unique abilities. Maslow described it as follows: Self Actualization is the intrinsic growth of what is already in the organism, or more accurately, of what the organism is.
Motivation	In psychology, motivation is the driving force (desire) behind all actions of an organism.
Humanistic	Humanistic refers to any system of thought focused on subjective experience and human problems and potentials.
Maslow	Maslow is mostly noted today for his proposal of a hierarchy of human needs which he often presented as a pyramid. Maslow was an instrumental player in the formation of the humanistic movement, also known as the third force in psychology.
Society	The social sciences use the term society to mean a group of people that form a semi-closed (or semi-open) social system, in which most interactions are with other individuals belonging to the group.
Cultural values	The importance and desirability of various objects and activities as defined by people in a given culture are referred to as cultural values.

Go to **Cram101.com** for the Practice Tests for this Chapter.

183

Personality trait	According to the Diagnostic and Statistical Manual of the American Psychiatric Association, a personality trait is a "prominent aspect of personality that is exhibited in a wide range of important social and personal contexts. ...".
Variable	A variable refers to a measurable factor, characteristic, or attribute of an individual or a system.
Incivility	Incivility is a general term for social behavior lacking in good manners, on a scale from lack of respect for elders, to vandalism and hooliganism, through public drunkenness and threatening behavior.
Modeling	A type of behavior learned through observation of others demonstrating the same behavior is modeling.
Sensation	Sensation is the first stage in the chain of biochemical and neurologic events that begins with the impinging of a stimulus upon the receptor cells of a sensory organ, which then leads to perception, the mental state that is reflected in statements like "I see a uniformly blue wall."
Adler	Adler argued that human personality could be explained teleologically, separate strands dominated by the guiding purpose of the individual's unconscious self ideal to convert feelings of inferiority to superiority (or rather completeness). The desires of the self ideal were countered by social and ethical demands.
Insecure attachment	Insecure attachment occurs when infants either avoid the caregiver or show considerable resistance or ambivalence toward the caregiver.
Object relation	Object relation theory is the idea that the ego-self exists only in relation to other objects, which may be external or internal.
Ambivalence	The simultaneous holding of strong positive and negative emotional attitudes toward the same situation or person is called ambivalence.
Self-esteem	Self-esteem refers to a person's subjective appraisal of himself or herself as intrinsically positive or negative to some degree.
Attachment	Attachment is the tendency to seek closeness to another person and feel secure when that person is present.
Agreeableness	Agreeableness, one of the big-five personality traits, reflects individual differences in concern with cooperation and social harmony. It is the degree individuals value getting along with others.
Extraversion	Extraversion, one of the big-five personailty traits, is marked by pronounced engagement with the external world. They are people who enjoy being with people, are full of energy, and often experience positive emotions.
Allport	Allport was a trait theorist. Those traits he believed to predominate a person's personality were called central traits. Traits such that one could be indentifed by the trait, were referred to as cardinal traits. Central traits and cardinal traits are influenced by environmental factors.
Heredity	Heredity is the transfer of characteristics from parent to offspring through their genes.
Chronic	Chronic refers to a relatively long duration, usually more than a few months.
Conformity	Conformity is the degree to which members of a group will change their behavior, views and attitudes to fit the views of the group. The group can influence members via unconscious processes or via overt social pressure on individuals.
Prototype	A concept of a category of objects or events that serves as a good example of the category is

Go to **Cram101.com** for the Practice Tests for this Chapter.

called a prototype.

Social learning theory	Social learning theory explains the process of gender typing in terms of observation, imitation, and role playing .
Self-efficacy	Self-efficacy is the belief that one has the capabilities to execute the courses of actions required to manage prospective situations.
Population	Population refers to all members of a well-defined group of organisms, events, or things.
Self-Regulatory	Bandura proposes that self-regulatory systems mediate external influences and provide a basis for purposeful action, allowing people to have personal control over their own thoughts, feelings, motivations, and actions.
Life stages	Widely recognized periods of life corresponding to broad phases of development are called life stages. They may cross-culturally or socially defined.
Stages	Stages represent relatively discrete periods of time in which functioning is qualitatively different from functioning at other periods.
Child development	Scientific study of the processes of change from conception through adolescence is called child development.
Adaptation	Adaptation is a lowering of sensitivity to a stimulus following prolonged exposure to that stimulus. Behavioral adaptations are special ways a particular organism behaves to survive in its natural habitat.
Phobia	A persistent, irrational fear of an object, situation, or activity that the person feels compelled to avoid is referred to as a phobia.
Cognitive learning	Higher-level learning involving thinking, knowing, understanding, and anticipation is cognitive learning.
Individual differences	Individual differences psychology studies the ways in which individual people differ in their behavior. This is distinguished from other aspects of psychology in that although psychology is ostensibly a study of individuals, modern psychologists invariably study groups.
Predisposition	Predisposition refers to an inclination or diathesis to respond in a certain way, either inborn or acquired. In abnormal psychology, it is a factor that lowers the ability to withstand stress and inclines the individual toward pathology.
Psychodynamic	Most psychodynamic approaches are centered around the idea of a maladapted function developed early in life (usually childhood) which are at least in part unconscious. This maladapted function (a.k.a. defense mechanism) does not do well in place of a normal/healthy one.
Paradigm	Paradigm refers to the set of practices that defines a scientific discipline during a particular period of time. It provides a framework from which to conduct research, it ensures that a certain range of phenomena, those on which the paradigm focuses, are explored thoroughly. Itmay also blind scientists to other, perhaps more fruitful, ways of dealing with their subject matter.
Variability	Statistically, variability refers to how much the scores in a distribution spread out, away from the mean.
Conscientiou-ness	Conscientiousness is one of the dimensions of the five-factor model of personality and individual differences involving being organized, thorough, and reliable as opposed to careless, negligent, and unreliable.
Intuition	Quick, impulsive thought that does not make use of formal logic or clear reasoning is referred to as intuition.
Empirical	Empirical means the use of working hypotheses which are capable of being disproved using

	observation or experiment.
Longitudinal research	Research that studies the same subjects over an extended period of time, usually several years or more, is called longitudinal research.
Punishment	Punishment is the addtion of a stimulus that reduces the frequency of a response, or the removal of a stimulus that results in a reduction of the response.
Introversion	A personality trait characterized by intense imagination and a tendency to inhibit impulses is called introversion.
Affect	A subjective feeling or emotional tone often accompanied by bodily expressions noticeable to others is called affect.
Psychological situation	A psychological situation refers to situation as it is perceived and interpreted by an individual, not necessarily as it exists objectively.
Perception	Perception is the process of acquiring, interpreting, selecting, and organizing sensory information.
Temperament	Temperament refers to a basic, innate disposition to change behavior. The activity level is an important dimension of temperament.
Toddler	A toddler is a child between the ages of one and three years old. During this period, the child learns a great deal about social roles and develops motor skills; to toddle is to walk unsteadily.
Genetics	Genetics is the science of genes, heredity, and the variation of organisms.
Encoding	Encoding refers to interpreting; transforming; modifying information so that it can be placed in memory. It is the first stage of information processing.
Reasoning	Reasoning is the act of using reason to derive a conclusion from certain premises. There are two main methods to reach a conclusion,deductive reasoning and inductive reasoning.
Discriminative stimulus	In operant conditioning, a stimulus that indicates that reinforcement is available upon the apporpriate response, is called the discriminative stimulus.
Skinner box	An operant conditioning chamber, or Skinner box, is an experimental apparatus used to study conditioning in animals. Chambers have at least one operandum that can automatically detect the occurrence of a behavioral response or action. The other minimal requirement of a conditioning chamber is that it have a means of delivering a primary reinforcer or unconditioned stimulus like food or water.
Stimulus	A change in an environmental condition that elicits a response is a stimulus.
Personality type	A persistent style of complex behaviors defined by a group of related traits is referred to as a personality type. Myer Friedman and his co-workers first defined personality types in the 1950s. Friedman classified people into 2 categories, Type A and Type B.
Romantic love	An intense, positive emotion that involves sexual attraction, feelings of caring, and the belief that one is in love is romantic love.
Stereotype	A stereotype is considered to be a group concept, held by one social group about another.They are often used in a negative or prejudicial sense and are frequently used to justify certain discriminatory behaviors. This allows powerful social groups to legitimize and protect their dominant position
Stimulus control	Linking a particular response with specific stimuli is called stimulus control.
Wisdom	Wisdom is the ability to make correct judgments and decisions. It is an intangible quality gained through experience. Whether or not something is wise is determined in a pragmatic

Go to **Cram101.com** for the Practice Tests for this Chapter.

189

sense by its popularity, how long it has been around, and its ability to predict against future events.

Attention deficit hyperactivity disorder	A learning disability marked by inattention, impulsiveness, a low tolerance for frustration, and a great deal of inappropriate activity is the attention deficit hyperactivity disorder.
Hyperactivity	Hyperactivity can be described as a state in which a individual is abnormally easily excitable and exuberant. Strong emotional reactions and a very short span of attention is also typical for the individual.
Psychoanalytic	Freud's theory that unconscious forces act as determinants of personality is called psychoanalytic theory. The theory is a developmental theory characterized by critical stages of development.
Reinforcer	In operant conditioning, a reinforcer is any stimulus that increases the probability that a preceding behavior will occur again. In Classical Conditioning, the unconditioned stimulus (US) is the reinforcer.
Frontal lobe	The frontal lobe comprises four major folds of cortical tissue: the precentral gyrus, superior gyrus and the middle gyrus of the frontal gyri, the inferior frontal gyrus. It has been found to play a part in impulse control, judgement, language, memory, motor function, problem solving, sexual behavior, socialization and spontaneity.
Hippocampus	The hippocampus is a part of the brain located inside the temporal lobe. It forms a part of the limbic system and plays a part in memory and navigation.
Amygdala	Located in the brain's medial temporal lobe, the almond-shaped amygdala is believed to play a key role in the emotions. It forms part of the limbic system and is linked to both fear responses and pleasure. Its size is positively correlated with aggressive behavior across species.
Brain	The brain controls and coordinates most movement, behavior and homeostatic body functions such as heartbeat, blood pressure, fluid balance and body temperature. Functions of the brain are responsible for cognition, emotion, memory, motor learning and other sorts of learning. The brain is primarily made up of two types of cells: glia and neurons.
Lobes	The four major sections of the cerebral cortex: frontal, parietal, temporal, and occipital are called lobes.
Schematic representation	The representation of objects in terms of real or potential interactions with other objects is called a schematic representation.
Behavioral model	Explanation of human behavior, including dysfunction, based on principles of learning and adaptation derived from experimental psychology is referred to as a behavioral model.
Cognitive structure	According to Piaget, the number of schemata available to an organism at any given time constitutes that organism's cognitive structure. How the organism interacts with its environment depends on the current cognitive structure available. As the cognitive structure develops, new assimilations can occur.
American Psychological Association	The American Psychological Association is a professional organization representing psychology in the US. The mission statement is to "advance psychology as a science and profession and as a means of promoting health, education , and human welfare".
Applied psychology	The basic premise of applied psychology is the use of psychological principles and theories to overcome practical problems.
Sexually	Sexually transmitted disease is commonly transmitted between partners through some form of

Transmitted Disease	sexual activity, most commonly vaginal intercourse, oral sex, or anal sex.
Role-playing	Role-playing refers to a technique that teaches people to behave in a certain way by encouraging them to pretend that they are in a particular situation; it helps people acquire complex behaviors in an efficient way.
Zimbardo	Zimbardo is best-known for his Stanford prison experiment. The experiment led to theories about the importance of the social situation in individual psychology that are still controversial today.
Fisher	Fisher was a eugenicist, evolutionary biologist, geneticist and statistician. He has been described as "The greatest of Darwin's successors", and a genius who almost single-handedly created the foundations for modern statistical science inventing the techniques of maximum likelihood and analysis of variance.
Survey	A method of scientific investigation in which a large sample of people answer questions about their attitudes or behavior is referred to as a survey.
Depression	In everyday language depression refers to any downturn in mood, which may be relatively transitory and perhaps due to something trivial. This is differentiated from Clinical depression which is marked by symptoms that last two weeks or more and are so severe that they interfere with daily living.
Proximal	Students can set both long-term (distal) and short-term (proximal) goals .
Autonomic nervous system	A division of the peripheral nervous system, the autonomic nervous system, regulates glands and activities such as heartbeat, respiration, digestion, and dilation of the pupils. It is responsible for homeostasis, maintaining a relatively constant internal environment .
Nervous system	The body's electrochemical communication circuitry, made up of billions of neurons is a nervous system.
Norepinephrine	Norepinephrine is released from the adrenal glands as a hormone into the blood, but it is also a neurotransmitter in the nervous system. As a stress hormone, it affects parts of the human brain where attention and impulsivity are controlled. Along with epinephrine, this compound effects the fight-or-flight response, activating the sympathetic nervous system to directly increase heart rate, release energy from fat, and increase muscle readiness.
Immune system	The most important function of the human immune system occurs at the cellular level of the blood and tissues. The lymphatic and blood circulation systems are highways for specialized white blood cells. These cells include B cells, T cells, natural killer cells, and macrophages. All function with the primary objective of recognizing, attacking and destroying bacteria, viruses, cancer cells, and all substances seen as foreign.
Epinephrine	Epinephrine is a hormone and a neurotransmitter. Epinephrine plays a central role in the short-term stress reaction—the physiological response to threatening or exciting conditions. It is secreted by the adrenal medulla. When released into the bloodstream, epinephrine binds to multiple receptors and has numerous effects throughout the body.
Opioid	An opioid is any agent that binds to opioid receptors, found principally in the central nervous system and gastrointestinal tract.
Experimental manipulation	The change that an experimenter deliberately produces in a situation under study is called the experimental manipulation.
Shaping	The concept of reinforcing successive, increasingly accurate approximations to a target behavior is called shaping. The target behavior is broken down into a hierarchy of elemental steps, each step more sophisticated then the last. By successively reinforcing each of the the elemental steps, a form of differential reinforcement, until that step is learned while

	extinguishing the step below, the target behavior is gradually achieved.
Gender role	A cluster of behaviors that characterizes traditional female or male behaviors within a cultural setting is a gender role.
Perceptual set	A predisposition or readiness to perceive something in a particular way is called a perceptual set.
Affective valence	In psychology and neuroscience, affective valence refers to the emotional value associated with a stimulus; e.g., a familiar face can have positive valence.
Affective	Affective is the way people react emotionally, their ability to feel another living thing's pain or joy.
Valence	In expectancy theory, the value or worth a person gives to an outcome is called the valence.
Motor reproduction	Motor reproduction involves converting symbolic representation into overt behavior and is essential for effective observational learning.
Coding	In senation, coding is the process by which information about the quality and quantity of a stimulus is preserved in the pattern of action potentials sent through sensory neurons to the central nervous system.
Motivational processes	In observational learning, the motivational processes are the degree to which a behavior is seen to result in a valued outcome (expectancies) will influence the likelihood that one will adopt a modeled behavior .
Feedback	Feedback refers to information returned to a person about the effects a response has had.
Vicarious reinforcement	A behavior response that increases as a result of observing other people's behaviors being reinforced is referred to as vicarious reinforcement.
Social cognitive theory	Social cognitive theory defines human behavior as a triadic, dynamic, and reciprocal interaction of personal factors, behavior, and the environment. Response consequences of a behavior are used to form expectations of behavioral outcomes. It is the ability to form these expectations that give humans the capability to predict the outcomes of their behavior, before the behavior is performed.
Neal Miller	Neal Miller introduced the concepts of the approach gradient and avoidance gradient. Whether organisms drive toward or away from a positive stimulus or a negative stimulus is a function of the distance that it is from that stimulus.
Necessary condition	A circumstance required for a particular phenomenon to occur is a necessary condition if and only if the condition does not occur in the absense of the circumstance.
Incentive	An incentive is what is expected once a behavior is performed. An incentive acts as a reinforcer.
Observational learning	The acquisition of knowledge and skills through the observation of others rather than by means of direct experience is observational learning. Four major processes are thought to influence the observational learning: attentional, retentional, behavioral production, and motivational.
Imitative learning	Imitative learning occurs when the learner internalizes something of a model's behavioral strategies. In Tomasello's theory of cultural learning, imitative learning is the first stage of cultural learning.
Vicarious learning	Vicarious learning is learning without specific reinforcement for one's behavior. It is learning by observing others.
Moral reasoning	Moral reasoning involves concepts of justice, whereas social conventional judgments are concepts of social organization.

195

Control group	A group that does not receive the treatment effect in an experiment is referred to as the control group or sometimes as the comparison group.
Bobo doll	The Bobo doll experiment was conducted by Bandura to study aggressive patterns of behavior. One of the experiment's conclusions was that people can learn through vicarious reinforcement.
Hormone	A hormone is a chemical messenger from one cell (or group of cells) to another. The best known are those produced by endocrine glands, but they are produced by nearly every organ system. The function of hormones is to serve as a signal to the target cells; the action of the hormone is determined by the pattern of secretion and the signal transduction of the receiving tissue.
Reinforcement contingencies	The circumstances or rules that determine whether responses lead to the presentation of reinforcers are referred to as reinforcement contingencies. Skinner defined culture as a set of reinforcement contingencies.
Acquisition	Acquisition is the process of adapting to the environment, learning or becoming conditioned. In classical conditoning terms, it is the initial learning of the stimulus response link, which involves a neutral stimulus being associated with a unconditioned stimulus and becoming a conditioned stimulus.
Discrimination	In Learning theory, discrimination refers the ability to distinguish between a conditioned stimulus and other stimuli. It can be brought about by extensive training or differential reinforcement. In social terms, it is the denial of privileges to a person or a group on the basis of prejudice.
Extinction	In operant extinction, if no reinforcement is delivered after the response, gradually the behavior will no longer occur in the presence of the stimulus. The process is more rapid following continuous reinforcement rather than after partial reinforcement. In Classical Conditioning, repeated presentations of the CS without being followed by the US results in the extinction of the CS.
Self-efficacy expectations	Beliefs to the effect that one can handle a task, that one can bring about desired changes through one's own efforts are called self-efficacy expectations.
Psychoanalysis	Psychoanalysis refers to the school of psychology that emphasizes the importance of unconscious motives and conflicts as determinants of human behavior. It was Freud's method of exploring human personality.
Individualism	Individualism refers to putting personal goals ahead of group goals and defining one's identity in terms of personal attributes rather than group memberships.
Psychoanalytic theory	Psychoanalytic theory is a general term for approaches to psychoanalysis which attempt to provide a conceptual framework more-or-less independent of clinical practice rather than based on empirical analysis of clinical cases.
Trait theory	According to trait theory, personality can be broken down into a limited number of traits, which are present in each individual to a greater or lesser degree. This approach is highly compatible with the quantitative psychometric approach to personality testing.
Psychoanalyst	A psychoanalyst is a specially trained therapist who attempts to treat the individual by uncovering and revealing to the individual otherwise subconscious factors that are contributing to some undesirable behavior.
Attentional processes	In Bandura's theory of vicarious learning, any activity by an observer that aids in the observation of relevant aspects of a model's behavior and its consequences is referred to as attentional processes.

Go to **Cram101.com** for the Practice Tests for this Chapter.

Achievement motivation	The psychological need in humans for success is called achievement motivation.
Motivation	In psychology, motivation is the driving force (desire) behind all actions of an organism.
Ego	In Freud's view the Ego serves to balance our primitive needs and our moral beliefs and taboos. Relying on experience, a healthy Ego provides the ability to adapt to reality and interact with the outside world.
Construct	A generalized concept, such as anxiety or gravity, is a construct.
Pragmatism	Pragmatism is characterized by the insistence on consequences, utility and practicality as vital components of truth. Pragmatism objects to the view that human concepts and intellect represent reality, and therefore stands in opposition to both formalist and rationalist schools of philosophy.
Social learning	Social learning is learning that occurs as a function of observing, retaining and replicating behavior observed in others. Although social learning can occur at any stage in life, it is thought to be particularly important during childhood, particularly as authority becomes important.
Learning	Learning is a relatively permanent change in behavior that results from experience. Thus, to attribute a behavioral change to learning, the change must be relatively permanent and must result from experience.
Personality	Personality refers to the pattern of enduring characteristics that differentiates a person, the patterns of behaviors that make each individual unique.
Coding	In senation, coding is the process by which information about the quality and quantity of a stimulus is preserved in the pattern of action potentials sent through sensory neurons to the central nervous system.
Idiographic	An idiographic investigation studies the characteristics of an individual in depth.
Nomothetic	Nomothetic measures are contrasted to ipsative or idiothetic measures, where nomothetic measures are measures that can be taken directly by an outside observer, such as weight or how many times a particular behavior occurs, and ipsative measures are self-reports such as a rank-ordered list of preferences.
George Kelly	George Kelly developed his major contribution to the psychology of personality, The Psychology of Personal Constructs in 1955 and achieved immediate international recognition. He worked in clinical school psychology, developing a program of traveling clinics which also served as a training ground for his students.
Cognitive revolution	The cognitive revolution is a name for an intellectual movement in the 1950s that combined new thinking in psychology, anthropology and linguistics with the nascent fields of computer science and neuroscience. In psychology, the movement was a response to behaviorism.
Cognition	The intellectual processes through which information is obtained, transformed, stored, retrieved, and otherwise used is cognition.
Variable	A variable refers to a measurable factor, characteristic, or attribute of an individual or a system.
Theories	Theories are logically self-consistent models or frameworks describing the behavior of a certain natural or social phenomenon. They are broad explanations and predictions concerning phenomena of interest.
Adler	Adler argued that human personality could be explained teleologically, separate strands dominated by the guiding purpose of the individual's unconscious self ideal to convert feelings of inferiority to superiority (or rather completeness). The desires of the self

Go to Cram101.com for the Practice Tests for this Chapter.

	ideal were countered by social and ethical demands.
Adaptation	Adaptation is a lowering of sensitivity to a stimulus following prolonged exposure to that stimulus. Behavioral adaptations are special ways a particular organism behaves to survive in its natural habitat.
Attention	Attention is the cognitive process of selectively concentrating on one thing while ignoring other things. Psychologists have labeled three types of attention: sustained attention, selective attention, and divided attention.
Clinical psychology	Clinical psychology is involved in the diagnosis, assessment, and treatment of patients with mental or behavioral disorders, and conducts research in these various areas.
Depression	In everyday language depression refers to any downturn in mood, which may be relatively transitory and perhaps due to something trivial. This is differentiated from Clinical depression which is marked by symptoms that last two weeks or more and are so severe that they interfere with daily living.
Metaphor	A metaphor is a rhetorical trope where a comparison is made between two seemingly unrelated subjects
Carl Rogers	Carl Rogers was instrumental in the development of non-directive psychotherapy, also known as "client-centered" psychotherapy. Rogers' basic tenets were unconditional positive regard, genuineness, and empathic understanding, with each demonstrated by the counselor.
Clinician	A health professional authorized to provide services to people suffering from one or more pathologies is a clinician.
Anxiety	Anxiety is a complex combination of the feeling of fear, apprehension and worry often accompanied by physical sensations such as palpitations, chest pain and/or shortness of breath.
Kuhn	Kuhn is most famous for his book The Structure of Scientific Revolutions in which he presented the idea that science does not evolve gradually toward truth, but instead undergoes periodic revolutions which he calls "paradigm shifts."
Friendship	The essentials of friendship are reciprocity and commitment between individuals who see themselves more or less as equals. Interaction between friends rests on a more equal power base than the interaction between children and adults.
Human nature	Human nature is the fundamental nature and substance of humans, as well as the range of human behavior that is believed to be invariant over long periods of time and across very different cultural contexts.
Hypothesis	A specific statement about behavior or mental processes that is testable through research is a hypothesis.
Bruner	Bruner has had an enormous impact on educational psychology with his contributions to cognitive learning theory. His ideas are based on categorization, maintaining that people interpret the world in terms of its similarities and differences.
Emotion	An emotion is a mental states that arise spontaneously, rather than through conscious effort. They are often accompanied by physiological changes.
Psychosomatic	A psychosomatic illness is one with physical manifestations and perhaps a supposed psychological cause. It is often diagnosed when any known or identifiable physical cause was excluded by medical examination.
Stages	Stages represent relatively discrete periods of time in which functioning is qualitatively different from functioning at other periods.

Elaboration	The extensiveness of processing at any given level of memory is called elaboration. The use of elaboration changes developmentally. Adolescents are more likely to use elaboration spontaneously than children.
Addiction	Addiction is an uncontrollable compulsion to repeat a behavior regardless of its consequences. Many drugs or behaviors can precipitate a pattern of conditions recognized as addiction, which include a craving for more of the drug or behavior, increased physiological tolerance to exposure, and withdrawal symptoms in the absence of the stimulus.
Dichotomy	A dichotomy is the division of a proposition into two parts which are both mutually exclusive – i.e. both cannot be simultaneously true – and jointly exhaustive – i.e. they cover the full range of possible outcomes. They are often contrasting and spoken of as "opposites".
Superordinate	A hypernym is a word whose extension includes the extension of the word of which it is a hypernym. A word that is more generic or broad than another given word. Another term for a hypernym is a superordinate.
Cholesterol	Cholesterol is a steroid, a lipid, and an alcohol, found in the cell membranes of all body tissues, and transported in the blood plasma of all animals. Cholesterol is an important component of the membranes of cells, providing stability; it makes the membrane's fluidity stable over a bigger temperature interval.
Individuality	According to Cooper, individuality consists of two dimensions: self-assertion and separateness.
Individual differences	Individual differences psychology studies the ways in which individual people differ in their behavior. This is distinguished from other aspects of psychology in that although psychology is ostensibly a study of individuals, modern psychologists invariably study groups.
Psychotherapy	Psychotherapy is a set of techniques based on psychological principles intended to improve mental health, emotional or behavioral issues.
Guthrie	The theory of learning proposed by Guthrie was based on one principle, Contiguity : A combination of stimuli which has accompanied a movement will on its recurrence tend to be followed by that movement. Prediction of behavior will always be probabilistic.
Counselor	A counselor is a mental health professional who specializes in helping people with problems not involving serious mental disorders.
Insight	Insight refers to a sudden awareness of the relationships among various elements that had previously appeared to be independent of one another.
Empirical	Empirical means the use of working hypotheses which are capable of being disproved using observation or experiment.
Suicide	Suicide behavior is rare in childhood but escalates in adolescence. The suicide rate increases in a linear fashion from adolescence through late adulthood.
Guilt	Guilt describes many concepts related to a negative emotion or condition caused by actions which are believed to be, morally wrong. According to Freud, the avoidance of guilt is the basis for moral behavior.
Dependent variable	A measure of an assumed effect of an independent variable is called the dependent variable.
Creativity	Creativity is the ability to think about something in novel and unusual ways and come up with unique solutions to problems. It involves divergent thinking, having many solutions or views to a problem.
Defense mechanism	A Defense mechanism is a set of unconscious ways to protect one's personality from unpleasant thoughts and realities which may otherwise cause anxiety. The notion is an integral part of

Go to **Cram101.com** for the Practice Tests for this Chapter.

	the psychoanalytic theory.
Rationalization	Rationalization is the process of constructing a logical justification for a decision that was originally arrived at through a different mental process. It is one of Freud's defense mechanisms.
Denial	Denial is a psychological defense mechanism in which a person faced with a fact that is uncomfortable or painful to accept rejects it instead, insisting that it is not true despite what may be overwhelming evidence.
Free association	In psychoanalysis, the uncensored uttering of all thoughts that come to mind is called free association.
Problem solving	An attempt to find an appropriate way of attaining a goal when the goal is not readily available is called problem solving.
Brainstorming	Brainstorming is an organized approach for producing ideas by letting the mind think without interruption. The term was coined by Alex Osborn.
Population	Population refers to all members of a well-defined group of organisms, events, or things.
Role-playing	Role-playing refers to a technique that teaches people to behave in a certain way by encouraging them to pretend that they are in a particular situation; it helps people acquire complex behaviors in an efficient way.
Attitude	An enduring mental representation of a person, place, or thing that evokes an emotional response and related behavior is called attitude.
Social constructionism	The focus of social constructionism is to uncover the ways in which individuals and groups participate in the creation of their perceived reality. As an approach, it involves looking at the ways social phenomena are created, institutionalized, and made into tradition by humans.
Constructivism	The view that individuals actively construct knowledge and understanding is referred to as constructivism.
Personality trait	According to the Diagnostic and Statistical Manual of the American Psychiatric Association, a personality trait is a "prominent aspect of personality that is exhibited in a wide range of important social and personal contexts. ...".
Trait	An enduring personality characteristic that tends to lead to certain behaviors is called a trait. The term trait also means a genetically inherited feature of an organism.

Humanistic psychology	Humanistic psychology refers to the school of psychology that focuses on the uniqueness of human beings and their capacity for choice, growth, and psychological health.
George Kelly	George Kelly developed his major contribution to the psychology of personality, The Psychology of Personal Constructs in 1955 and achieved immediate international recognition. He worked in clinical school psychology, developing a program of traveling clinics which also served as a training ground for his students.
Henry Murray	Henry Murray believed that personality could be better understood by investigating the unconscious mind. He is most famous for the development of the Thematic Apperception Test (TAT), a widely used projective measure of personality.
Carl Rogers	Carl Rogers was instrumental in the development of non-directive psychotherapy, also known as "client-centered" psychotherapy. Rogers' basic tenets were unconditional positive regard, genuineness, and empathic understanding, with each demonstrated by the counselor.
Humanistic	Humanistic refers to any system of thought focused on subjective experience and human problems and potentials.
Wertheimer	His discovery of the phi phenomenon concerning the illusion of motion gave rise to the influential school of Gestalt psychology. In the latter part of his life, Wertheimer directed much of his attention to the problem of learning.
Rollo May	Rollo May was the best known American existential psychologist, authoring the influential book Love and Will in 1969. He differs from other humanistic psychologists in showing a sharper awareness of the tragic dimensions of human existence.
Allport	Allport was a trait theorist. Those traits he believed to predominate a person's personality were called central traits. Traits such that one could be indentifed by the trait, were referred to as cardinal traits. Central traits and cardinal traits are influenced by environmental factors.
Maslow	Maslow is mostly noted today for his proposal of a hierarchy of human needs which he often presented as a pyramid. Maslow was an instrumental player in the formation of the humanistic movement, also known as the third force in psychology.
Trait	An enduring personality characteristic that tends to lead to certain behaviors is called a trait. The term trait also means a genetically inherited feature of an organism.
Adler	Adler argued that human personality could be explained teleologically, separate strands dominated by the guiding purpose of the individual's unconscious self ideal to convert feelings of inferiority to superiority (or rather completeness). The desires of the self ideal were countered by social and ethical demands.
Subjective experience	Subjective experience refers to reality as it is perceived and interpreted, not as it exists objectively.
Creativity	Creativity is the ability to think about something in novel and unusual ways and come up with unique solutions to problems. It involves divergent thinking, having many solutions or views to a problem.
Humanistic perspective	The approach that suggests that all individuals naturally strive to grow, develop, and be in control of their lives and behavior is called the humanistic perspective.
Self-reflection	In Bandura's social cognitive theory, the ability to analyze one's thoughts and actions is referred to as self-reflection.
Socialization	Social rules and social relations are created, communicated, and changed in verbal and nonverbal ways creating social complexity useful in identifying outsiders and intelligent breeding partners. The process of learning these skills is called socialization.

Go to **Cram101.com** for the Practice Tests for this Chapter.

Self-actualization	Self-actualization (a term originated by Kurt Goldstein) is the instinctual need of a human to make the most of their unique abilities. Maslow described it as follows: Self Actualization is the intrinsic growth of what is already in the organism, or more accurately, of what the organism is.
Self-disclosure	The process of revealing private thoughts, feelings, and one's personal history to others is referred to as self-disclosure.
Individualism	Individualism refers to putting personal goals ahead of group goals and defining one's identity in terms of personal attributes rather than group memberships.
Aristotle	Aristotle can be credited with the development of the first theory of learning. He concluded that ideas were generated in consciousness based on four principlesof association: contiguity, similarity, contrast, and succession. In contrast to Plato, he believed that knowledge derived from sensory experience and was not inherited.
Humanism	Humanism refers to the philosophy and school of psychology that asserts that people are conscious, self-aware, and capable of free choice, self-fulfillment, and ethical behavior.
Ideology	An ideology can be thought of as a comprehensive vision, as a way of looking at things, as in common sense and several philosophical tendencies, or a set of ideas proposed by the dominant class of a society to all members of this society.
Individual differences	Individual differences psychology studies the ways in which individual people differ in their behavior. This is distinguished from other aspects of psychology in that although psychology is ostensibly a study of individuals, modern psychologists invariably study groups.
Teleology	While science investigates natural laws and phenomena, Philosophical naturalism and teleology investigate the existence or non-existence of an organizing principle behind those natural laws and phenonema. Philosophical naturalism asserts that there are no such principles. Teleology asserts that there are.
Logical positivism	Logical positivism holds that philosophy should aspire to the same sort of rigor as science. Philosophy should provide strict criteria for judging sentences true, false and meaningless.
Determinism	Determinism is the philosophical proposition that every event, including human cognition and action, is causally determined by an unbroken chain of prior occurrences.
Positivism	Positivism is an approach to understanding the world based on science. It can be traced back to Auguste Comte in the 19th century. Positivists believe that there is little if any methodological difference between social sciences and natural sciences; societies, like nature, operate according to laws.
Csikszentmihalyi	Csikszentmihalyi is noted for his work in the study of happiness, creativity, subjective well-being, and fun, but is best known for his having been the architect of the notion of flow: "... people are most happy when they are in a state of flow--a Zen-like state of total oneness...".
Empirical	Empirical means the use of working hypotheses which are capable of being disproved using observation or experiment.
Scientific method	Psychologists gather data in order to describe, understand, predict, and control behavior. Scientific method refers to an approach that can be used to discover accurate information. It includes these steps: understand the problem, collect data, draw conclusions, and revise research conclusions.
Adolescence	The period of life bounded by puberty and the assumption of adult responsibilities is adolescence.
Individuality	According to Cooper, individuality consists of two dimensions: self-assertion and

Go to **Cram101.com** for the Practice Tests for this Chapter.

	separateness.
Self-esteem	Self-esteem refers to a person's subjective appraisal of himself or herself as intrinsically positive or negative to some degree.
Sexism	Sexism is commonly considered to be discrimination against people based on their sex rather than their individual merits, but can also refer to any and all differentiations based on
Personality	Personality refers to the pattern of enduring characteristics that differentiates a person, the patterns of behaviors that make each individual unique.
Theories	Theories are logically self-consistent models or frameworks describing the behavior of a certain natural or social phenomenon. They are broad explanations and predictions concerning phenomena of interest.
Mutism	Mutism refers to refusal or inability to talk.
Trauma	Trauma refers to a severe physical injury or wound to the body caused by an external force, or a psychological shock having a lasting effect on mental life.
Guilt	Guilt describes many concepts related to a negative emotion or condition caused by actions which are believed to be, morally wrong. According to Freud, the avoidance of guilt is the basis for moral behavior.
Jung	Jung was in some aspects a response to Sigmund Freud's psychoanalysis. He proposed and developed the concepts of the extroverted and introverted personality, archetypes, and the collective unconscious. His work has been influential in psychiatry and in the study of religion, literature, and related fields.
Reinforcement	In operant conditioning, reinforcement is any change in an environment that (a) occurs after the behavior, (b) seems to make that behavior re-occur more often in the future and (c) that reoccurence of behavior must be the result of the change.
Learning	Learning is a relatively permanent change in behavior that results from experience. Thus, to attribute a behavioral change to learning, the change must be relatively permanent and must result from experience.
Hypothesis	A specific statement about behavior or mental processes that is testable through research is a hypothesis.
Cognitive learning	Higher-level learning involving thinking, knowing, understanding, and anticipation is cognitive learning.
Bandura	Bandura is best known for his work on social learning theory or Social Cognitivism. His famous Bobo doll experiment illustrated that people learn from observing others.
Alcoholic	An alcoholic is dependent on alcohol as characterized by craving, loss of control, physical dependence and withdrawal symptoms, and tolerance.
Attention	Attention is the cognitive process of selectively concentrating on one thing while ignoring other things. Psychologists have labeled three types of attention: sustained attention, selective attention, and divided attention.
Death instinct	The death instinct was defined by Sigmund Freud, in Beyond the Pleasure Principle(1920). It speculated on the existence of a fundamental death wish or death instinct, referring to an individual's own need to die.
Instinct	Instinct is the word used to describe inherent dispositions towards particular actions. They are generally an inherited pattern of responses or reactions to certain kinds of situations.
Thanatos	In psychoanalytical theory, Thanatos is the death instinct, which opposes Eros. The "death instinct" identified by Sigmund Freud, which signals a desire to give up the struggle of life

Go to **Cram101.com** for the Practice Tests for this Chapter.

	and return to quiescence and the grave.
Eros	In Freudian psychology, Eros is the life instinct innate in all humans. It is the desire to create life and favours productivity and construction. Eros battles against the destructive death instinct of Thanatos.
Ego	In Freud's view the Ego serves to balance our primitive needs and our moral beliefs and taboos. Relying on experience, a healthy Ego provides the ability to adapt to reality and interact with the outside world.
Psychoanalytic	Freud's theory that unconscious forces act as determinants of personality is called psychoanalytic theory. The theory is a developmental theory characterized by critical stages of development.
Motivation	In psychology, motivation is the driving force (desire) behind all actions of an organism.
Stage theory	Stage theory characterizes development by hypothesizing the existence of distinct, and often critical, periods of life. Each period follows one another in an orderly sequence.
Stages	Stages represent relatively discrete periods of time in which functioning is qualitatively different from functioning at other periods.
Society	The social sciences use the term society to mean a group of people that form a semi-closed (or semi-open) social system, in which most interactions are with other individuals belonging to the group.
Object relation	Object relation theory is the idea that the ego-self exists only in relation to other objects, which may be external or internal.
Karen Horney	Karen Horney, a neo-Freudian, deviated from orthodox Freudian analysis by emphasizing environmental and cultural, rather than biological, factors in neurosis.
Generativity	Generativity refers to an adult's concern for and commitment to the well-being of future generations.
Nomothetic	Nomothetic measures are contrasted to ipsative or idiothetic measures, where nomothetic measures are measures that can be taken directly by an outside observer, such as weight or how many times a particular behavior occurs, and ipsative measures are self-reports such as a rank-ordered list of preferences.
Conscientiou-ness	Conscientiousness is one of the dimensions of the five-factor model of personality and individual differences involving being organized, thorough, and reliable as opposed to careless, negligent, and unreliable.
Sensation	Sensation is the first stage in the chain of biochemical and neurologic events that begins with the impinging of a stimulus upon the receptor cells of a sensory organ, which then leads to perception, the mental state that is reflected in statements like "I see a uniformly blue wall."
Anxiety	Anxiety is a complex combination of the feeling of fear, apprehension and worry often accompanied by physical sensations such as palpitations, chest pain and/or shortness of breath.
Shyness	A tendency to avoid others plus uneasiness and strain when socializing is called shyness.
Punishment	Punishment is the addtion of a stimulus that reduces the frequency of a response, or the removal of a stimulus that results in a reduction of the response.
Deprivation	Deprivation, is the loss or withholding of normal stimulation, nutrition, comfort, love, and so forth; a condition of lacking. The level of stimulation is less than what is required.
Reinforcer	In operant conditioning, a reinforcer is any stimulus that increases the probability that a

preceding behavior will occur again. In Classical Conditioning, the unconditioned stimulus (US) is the reinforcer.

Behavior modification	Behavior Modification is a technique of altering an individual's reactions to stimuli through positive reinforcement and the extinction of maladaptive behavior.
Habit	A habit is a response that has become completely separated from its eliciting stimulus. Early learning theorists used the term to describe S-R associations, however not all S-R associations become a habit, rather many are extinguished after reinforcement is withdrawn.
Social skills	Social skills are skills used to interact and communicate with others to assist status in the social structure and other motivations.
Social learning	Social learning is learning that occurs as a function of observing, retaining and replicating behavior observed in others. Although social learning can occur at any stage in life, it is thought to be particularly important during childhood, particularly as authority becomes important.
Construct	A generalized concept, such as anxiety or gravity, is a construct.
Overt behavior	An action or response that is directly observable and measurable is an overt behavior.
Prejudice	Prejudice in general, implies coming to a judgment on the subject before learning where the preponderance of the evidence actually lies, or formation of a judgement without direct experience.
Emotion	An emotion is a mental states that arise spontaneously, rather than through conscious effort. They are often accompanied by physiological changes.
Empathic understanding	Empathic understanding refers to ability to perceive a client's feelings from the client's frame of reference.
Ethnicity	Ethnicity refers to a characteristic based on cultural heritage, nationality characteristics, race, religion, and language.
Unconditional positive regard	Unqualified caring and nonjudgmental acceptance of another is called unconditional positive regard.
Attitude	An enduring mental representation of a person, place, or thing that evokes an emotional response and related behavior is called attitude.
Depression	In everyday language depression refers to any downturn in mood, which may be relatively transitory and perhaps due to something trivial. This is differentiated from Clinical depression which is marked by symptoms that last two weeks or more and are so severe that they interfere with daily living.
Juvenile delinquent	An adolescent who breaks the law or engages in behavior that is considered illegal is referred to as a juvenile delinquent.
Love withdrawal	A discipline technique in which a parent removes attention or love from a child is referred to as love withdrawal.
Humanistic theories	Humanistic theories focus attention on the whole, unique person, especially on the person's conscious understanding of his or her self and the world.
Child development	Scientific study of the processes of change from conception through adolescence is called child development.
Insight	Insight refers to a sudden awareness of the relationships among various elements that had previously appeared to be independent of one another.
Adaptation	Adaptation is a lowering of sensitivity to a stimulus following prolonged exposure to that

	stimulus. Behavioral adaptations are special ways a particular organism behaves to survive in its natural habitat.
Encounter group	A type of group that fosters self-awareness by focusing on how group members relate to one another in a setting that encourages open expression of feelings is called an encounter group.
Group therapy	Group therapy is a form of psychotherapy during which one or several therapists treat a small group of clients together as a group. This may be more cost effective than individual therapy, and possibly even more effective.
Therapeutic community	A concept in mental health care that views the total environment as contributing to prevention or treatment is referred to as the therapeutic community.
Client-Centered Therapy	Client-Centered Therapy was developed by Carl Rogers. It is based on the principal of talking therapy and is a non-directive approach. The therapist encourages the patient to express their feelings and does not suggest how the person might wish to change, but by listening and then mirroring back what the patient reveals to them, helps them to explore and understand their feelings for themselves.
Psychoanalysis	Psychoanalysis refers to the school of psychology that emphasizes the importance of unconscious motives and conflicts as determinants of human behavior. It was Freud's method of exploring human personality.
Self-actualizing	Self-actualizing is the need of a human to make the most of their unique abilities.
Innate	Innate behavior is not learned or influenced by the environment, rather, it is present or predisposed at birth.
Openness to Experience	Openness to Experience, one of the big-five traits, describes a dimension of cognitive style that distinguishes imaginative, creative people from down-to-earth, conventional people.
Evolution	Commonly used to refer to gradual change, evolution is the change in the frequency of alleles within a population from one generation to the next. This change may be caused by different mechanisms, including natural selection, genetic drift, or changes in population (gene flow).
Consciousness	The awareness of the sensations, thoughts, and feelings being experienced at a given moment is called consciousness.
Mischel	Mischel is known for his cognitive social learning model of personality that focuses on the specific cognitive variables that mediate the manner in which new experiences affect the individual.
Psychoanalytic theory	Psychoanalytic theory is a general term for approaches to psychoanalysis which attempt to provide a conceptual framework more-or-less independent of clinical practice rather than based on empirical analysis of clinical cases.
Defense mechanism	A Defense mechanism is a set of unconscious ways to protect one's personality from unpleasant thoughts and realities which may otherwise cause anxiety. The notion is an integral part of the psychoanalytic theory.
Authoritarian parents	Parents who are rigid in their rules and who demand obedience for the sake of obedience are called authoritarian parents.
Authoritarian	The term authoritarian is used to describe a style that enforces strong and sometimes oppressive measures against those in its sphere of influence, generally without attempts at gaining their consent.
Obedience	Obedience is the willingness to follow the will of others. Humans have been shown to be surprisingly obedient in the presence of perceived legitimate authority figures, as demonstrated by the Milgram experiment in the 1960s.

Go to Cram101.com for the Practice Tests for this Chapter.

Maladaptive	In psychology, a behavior or trait is adaptive when it helps an individual adjust and function well within their social environment. A maladaptive behavior or trait is counterproductive to the individual.
Self-understanding	Self-understanding is a child's cognitive representation of the self, the substance and content of the child's self-conceptions.
Medical model	The medical model views abnormal behavior as a disease.
Wisdom	Wisdom is the ability to make correct judgments and decisions. It is an intangible quality gained through experience. Whether or not something is wise is determined in a pragmatic sense by its popularity, how long it has been around, and its ability to predict against future events.
Sufficient condition	To say that A is a sufficient condition for B is to say precisely the converse: that A cannot occur without B, or whenever A occurs, B occurs. That there is a fire is sufficient for there being smoke.
Psychotherapy	Psychotherapy is a set of techniques based on psychological principles intended to improve mental health, emotional or behavioral issues.
Empathy	Empathy is the recognition and understanding of the states of mind, including beliefs, desires and particularly emotions of others without injecting your own.
Perception	Perception is the process of acquiring, interpreting, selecting, and organizing sensory information.
Counselor	A counselor is a mental health professional who specializes in helping people with problems not involving serious mental disorders.
Skinner	Skinner conducted research on shaping behavior through positive and negative reinforcement, and demonstrated operant conditioning, a technique which he developed in contrast with classical conditioning.
Transference	Transference is a phenomenon in psychology characterized by unconscious redirection of feelings from one person to another.
Self-concept	Self-concept refers to domain-specific evaluations of the self where a domain may be academics, athletics, etc.
Lewin	Lewin ranks as one of the pioneers of social psychology, as one of the founders of group dynamics and as one of the most eminent representatives of Gestalt psychology.
Nurture	Nurture refers to the environmental influences on behavior due to nutrition, culture, socioeconomic status, and learning.
Educational technology	Educational Technology is a systematic, iterative process for designing instruction or training used to improve performance.
Values Clarification	Values clarification means helping people to clarify what their lives are for and what is worth working for. Values clarification differs from character education in not telling students what their values should be.
Gerontology	Gerontology is the study of the elderly, and of the aging process itself. It is to be distinguished from geriatrics, which is the study of the diseases of the elderly. Gerontology covers the social, psychological and biology aspects of aging.
Growth needs	Maslow's hierarchy of needs is often depicted as a pyramid consisting of five levels: the four lower levels are grouped together as deficiency needs, while the top level is termed growth needs, those of self-actualization.
Friendship	The essentials of friendship are reciprocity and commitment between individuals who see

themselves more or less as equals. Interaction between friends rests on a more equal power base than the interaction between children and adults.

Industrial-organizational psychology

Industrial-organizational psychology is the study of the behavior of people in the workplace. Industrial and organizational psychology attempts to apply psychological results and methods to aid workers and organizations.

Human nature

Human nature is the fundamental nature and substance of humans, as well as the range of human behavior that is believed to be invariant over long periods of time and across very different cultural contexts.

Survey

A method of scientific investigation in which a large sample of people answer questions about their attitudes or behavior is referred to as a survey.

American Psychological Association

The American Psychological Association is a professional organization representing psychology in the US. The mission statement is to "advance psychology as a science and profession and as a means of promoting health, education , and human welfare".

Free will

The idea that human beings are capable of freely making choices or decisions is free will.

220

Go to **Cram101.com** for the Practice Tests for this Chapter.

Hierarchy of needs	Maslow's hierarchy of needs is often depicted as a pyramid consisting of five levels: the four lower levels are grouped together as deficiency needs, while the top level is termed being needs. While our deficiency needs must be met, our being needs are continually shaping our behavior.
Maslow	Maslow is mostly noted today for his proposal of a hierarchy of human needs which he often presented as a pyramid. Maslow was an instrumental player in the formation of the humanistic movement, also known as the third force in psychology.
Self-actualization	Self-actualization (a term originated by Kurt Goldstein) is the instinctual need of a human to make the most of their unique abilities. Maslow described it as follows: Self Actualization is the intrinsic growth of what is already in the organism, or more accurately, of what the organism is.
Motivation	In psychology, motivation is the driving force (desire) behind all actions of an organism.
Instinct	Instinct is the word used to describe inherent dispositions towards particular actions. They are generally an inherited pattern of responses or reactions to certain kinds of situations.
Humanistic perspective	The approach that suggests that all individuals naturally strive to grow, develop, and be in control of their lives and behavior is called the humanistic perspective.
Humanistic	Humanistic refers to any system of thought focused on subjective experience and human problems and potentials.
Alcoholic	An alcoholic is dependent on alcohol as characterized by craving, loss of control, physical dependence and withdrawal symptoms, and tolerance.
Self-esteem	Self-esteem refers to a person's subjective appraisal of himself or herself as intrinsically positive or negative to some degree.
Subjective experience	Subjective experience refers to reality as it is perceived and interpreted, not as it exists objectively.
Deprivation	Deprivation, is the loss or withholding of normal stimulation, nutrition, comfort, love, and so forth; a condition of lacking. The level of stimulation is less than what is required.
Adaptation	Adaptation is a lowering of sensitivity to a stimulus following prolonged exposure to that stimulus. Behavioral adaptations are special ways a particular organism behaves to survive in its natural habitat.
Society	The social sciences use the term society to mean a group of people that form a semi-closed (or semi-open) social system, in which most interactions are with other individuals belonging to the group.
Personality	Personality refers to the pattern of enduring characteristics that differentiates a person, the patterns of behaviors that make each individual unique.
Intellectually gifted	Intellectually gifted refers to having an IQ score above 130; about 2 to 4 percent of the population.
Behaviorism	The school of psychology that defines psychology as the study of observable behavior and studies relationships between stimuli and responses is called behaviorism. Behaviorism relied heavily on animal research and stated the same principles governed the behavior of both nonhumans and humans.
Harlow	Harlow and his famous wire and cloth surrogate mother monkey studies demonstrated that the need for affection created a stronger bond between mother and infant than did physical needs. He also found that the more discrimination problems the monkeys solved, the better they became at solving them.

Go to **Cram101.com** for the Practice Tests for this Chapter.

Anxiety	Anxiety is a complex combination of the feeling of fear, apprehension and worry often accompanied by physical sensations such as palpitations, chest pain and/or shortness of breath.
Psychoanalysis	Psychoanalysis refers to the school of psychology that emphasizes the importance of unconscious motives and conflicts as determinants of human behavior. It was Freud's method of exploring human personality.
Psychotherapy	Psychotherapy is a set of techniques based on psychological principles intended to improve mental health, emotional or behavioral issues.
Insomnia	Insomnia is a sleep disorder characterized by an inability to sleep and/or to remain asleep for a reasonable period during the night.
Human nature	Human nature is the fundamental nature and substance of humans, as well as the range of human behavior that is believed to be invariant over long periods of time and across very different cultural contexts.
Theories	Theories are logically self-consistent models or frameworks describing the behavior of a certain natural or social phenomenon. They are broad explanations and predictions concerning phenomena of interest.
Allport	Allport was a trait theorist. Those traits he believed to predominate a person's personality were called central traits. Traits such that one could be indentifed by the trait, were referred to as cardinal traits. Central traits and cardinal traits are influenced by environmental factors.
Trait	An enduring personality characteristic that tends to lead to certain behaviors is called a trait. The term trait also means a genetically inherited feature of an organism.
Logical positivism	Logical positivism holds that philosophy should aspire to the same sort of rigor as science. Philosophy should provide strict criteria for judging sentences true, false and meaningless.
Determinism	Determinism is the philosophical proposition that every event, including human cognition and action, is causally determined by an unbroken chain of prior occurrences.
Positivism	Positivism is an approach to understanding the world based on science. It can be traced back to Auguste Comte in the 19th century. Positivists believe that there is little if any methodological difference between social sciences and natural sciences; societies, like nature, operate according to laws.
Clinician	A health professional authorized to provide services to people suffering from one or more pathologies is a clinician.
Existentialism	The view that people are completely free and responsible for their own behavior is existentialism.
Humanism	Humanism refers to the philosophy and school of psychology that asserts that people are conscious, self-aware, and capable of free choice, self-fulfillment, and ethical behavior.
Scientific method	Psychologists gather data in order to describe, understand, predict, and control behavior. Scientific method refers to an approach that can be used to discover accurate information. It includes these steps: understand the problem, collect data, draw conclusions, and revise research conclusions.
Emotion	An emotion is a mental states that arise spontaneously, rather than through conscious effort. They are often accompanied by physiological changes.
Defense mechanism	A Defense mechanism is a set of unconscious ways to protect one's personality from unpleasant thoughts and realities which may otherwise cause anxiety. The notion is an integral part of the psychoanalytic theory.

Go to **Cram101.com** for the Practice Tests for this Chapter.

Motives	Needs or desires that energize and direct behavior toward a goal are motives.
Basic research	Basic research has as its primary objective the advancement of knowledge and the theoretical understanding of the relations among variables . It is exploratory and often driven by the researcher's curiosity, interest or hunch.
Self-worth	In psychology, self-esteem or self-worth refers to a person's subjective appraisal of himself or herself as intrinsically positive or negative to some degree.
Regression	Return to a form of behavior characteristic of an earlier stage of development is called regression.
Empirical evidence	Facts or information based on direct observation or experience are referred to as empirical evidence.
Empirical	Empirical means the use of working hypotheses which are capable of being disproved using observation or experiment.
Physiological needs	The easiest kinds of motivation to analyse, at least superficially, are those based upon obvious physiological needs. These include hunger, thirst, and escape from pain.
Attention	Attention is the cognitive process of selectively concentrating on one thing while ignoring other things. Psychologists have labeled three types of attention: sustained attention, selective attention, and divided attention.
Neurosis	Neurosis, any mental disorder that, although may cause distress, does not interfere with rational thought or the persons' ability to function.
Brain	The brain controls and coordinates most movement, behavior and homeostatic body functions such as heartbeat, blood pressure, fluid balance and body temperature. Functions of the brain are responsible for cognition, emotion, memory, motor learning and other sorts of learning. The brain is primarily made up of two types of cells: glia and neurons.
Alfred Kinsey	Alfred Kinsey researched human sexuality and profoundly influenced social and cultural values in the United States especially in the 1960s and was an important influence on the sexual revolution
Homosexuality	Homosexuality refers to a sexual orientation characterized by aesthetic attraction, romantic love, and sexual desire exclusively for members of the same sex or gender identity.
Sexology	Sexology is the systematic study of human sexuality. It encompasses all aspects of sexuality, including attempting to characterise "normal sexuality" and its variants, including paraphilias.
Premise	A premise is a statement presumed true within the context of a discourse, especially of a logical argument.
Adler	Adler argued that human personality could be explained teleologically, separate strands dominated by the guiding purpose of the individual's unconscious self ideal to convert feelings of inferiority to superiority (or rather completeness). The desires of the self ideal were countered by social and ethical demands.
Deficiency needs	Maslow's hierarchy of needs is often depicted as a pyramid consisting of five levels: the four lower levels are grouped together as deficiency needs associated with physiological, safety, belonginess, and esteem needs.
Meta-needs	Abraham Maslow identified core values as meta-needs. These needs can't be permanently fulfilled.
Perception	Perception is the process of acquiring, interpreting, selecting, and organizing sensory information.

Go to Cram101.com for the Practice Tests for this Chapter.

Autonomy	Autonomy is the condition of something that does not depend on anything else.
Psychiatrist	A psychiatrist is a physician who specializes in the diagnosis and treatment of psychological disorders.
Suicide	Suicide behavior is rare in childhood but escalates in adolescence. The suicide rate increases in a linear fashion from adolescence through late adulthood.
Graham	Graham has conducted a number of studies that reveal stronger socioeconomic-status influences rather than ethnic influences in achievement.
Adolescence	The period of life bounded by puberty and the assumption of adult responsibilities is adolescence.
Locus of control	The place to which an individual attributes control over the receiving of reinforcers -either inside or outside the self is referred to as locus of control.
Neuroticism	Eysenck's use of the term neuroticism (or Emotional Stability) was proposed as the dimension describing individual differences in the predisposition towards neurotic disorder.
Depression	In everyday language depression refers to any downturn in mood, which may be relatively transitory and perhaps due to something trivial. This is differentiated from Clinical depression which is marked by symptoms that last two weeks or more and are so severe that they interfere with daily living.
Sullivan	Sullivan developed the Self System, a configuration of the personality traits developed in childhood and reinforced by positive affirmation and the security operations developed in childhood to avoid anxiety and threats to self-esteem.
Survey	A method of scientific investigation in which a large sample of people answer questions about their attitudes or behavior is referred to as a survey.
Evolution	Commonly used to refer to gradual change, evolution is the change in the frequency of alleles within a population from one generation to the next. This change may be caused by different mechanisms, including natural selection, genetic drift, or changes in population (gene flow).
Karen Horney	Karen Horney, a neo-Freudian, deviated from orthodox Freudian analysis by emphasizing environmental and cultural, rather than biological, factors in neurosis.
Self-actualizing	Self-actualizing is the need of a human to make the most of their unique abilities.
Stereotype	A stereotype is considered to be a group concept, held by one social group about another.They are often used in a negative or prejudicial sense and are frequently used to justify certain discriminatory behaviors. This allows powerful social groups to legitimize and protect their dominant position
Sensory deprivation	Sensory deprivation is the deliberate reduction or removal of stimuli from one or more of the senses. Though short periods of sensory deprivation can be relaxing, extended deprivation can result in extreme anxiety, hallucinations, bizarre thoughts, depression, and antisocial behavior.
Ecstasy	Ecstasy as an emotion is to be outside oneself, in a trancelike state in which an individual transcends ordinary consciousness and as a result has a heightened capacity for exceptional thought or experience. Ecstasy also refers to a relatively new hallucinogen that is chemically similar to mescaline and the amphetamines.
Meditation	Meditation usually refers to a state in which the body is consciously relaxed and the mind is allowed to become calm and focused.
Hypnotic susceptibility	One's capacity for becoming hypnotized is referred to as hypnotic susceptibility. People who are more easily put into a state of hypnosis are also more suggestible.

Go to **Cram101.com** for the Practice Tests for this Chapter.
And, **NEVER** highlight a book again!

Peak experiences	Temporary moments of self-actualization are peak experiences.
Consciousness	The awareness of the sensations, thoughts, and feelings being experienced at a given moment is called consciousness.
Ego	In Freud's view the Ego serves to balance our primitive needs and our moral beliefs and taboos. Relying on experience, a healthy Ego provides the ability to adapt to reality and interact with the outside world.
Psychoactive drug	A psychoactive drug or psychotropic substance is a chemical that alters brain function, resulting in temporary changes in perception, mood, consciousness, or behavior. Such drugs are often used for recreational and spiritual purposes, as well as in medicine, especially for treating neurological and psychological illnesses.
Insight	Insight refers to a sudden awareness of the relationships among various elements that had previously appeared to be independent of one another.
Discrimination	In Learning theory, discrimination refers the ability to distinguish between a conditioned stimulus and other stimuli. It can be brought about by extensive training or differential reinforcement. In social terms, it is the denial of privileges to a person or a group on the basis of prejudice.
Creativity	Creativity is the ability to think about something in novel and unusual ways and come up with unique solutions to problems. It involves divergent thinking, having many solutions or views to a problem.
Correlation	A statistical technique for determining the degree of association between two or more variables is referred to as correlation.
Secondary process	Secondary process is the mental activity and thinking characteristic of the ego, influenced by the demands of the environment. Characterized by organization, systematization, intellectualization, and similar processes leading to logical thought and action in adult life.
Psychoanalyst	A psychoanalyst is a specially trained therapist who attempts to treat the individual by uncovering and revealing to the individual otherwise subconscious factors that are contributing to some undesirable behavor.
Reasoning	Reasoning is the act of using reason to derive a conclusion from certain premises. There are two main methods to reach a conclusion,deductive reasoning and inductive reasoning.
Habit	A habit is a response that has become completely separated from its eliciting stimulus. Early learning theorists used the term to describe S-R associations, however not all S-R associations become a habit, rather many are extinguished after reinforcement is withdrawn.
Friendship	The essentials of friendship are reciprocity and commitment between individuals who see themselves more or less as equals. Interaction between friends rests on a more equal power base than the interaction between children and adults.
Nomothetic	Nomothetic measures are contrasted to ipsative or idiothetic measures, where nomothetic measures are measures that can be taken directly by an outside observer, such as weight or how many times a particular behavior occurs, and ipsative measures are self-reports such as a rank-ordered list of preferences.
Stages	Stages represent relatively discrete periods of time in which functioning is qualitatively different from functioning at other periods.
Questionnaire	A self-report method of data collection or clinical assessment method in which the individual being studied checks off items on a printed list, answers multiple-choice questions, or writes out answers to essay questions aimed at producing a selfdescription is called

	questionnaire.
Construct	A generalized concept, such as anxiety or gravity, is a construct.
Counseling psychologist	A doctoral level mental health professional whose training is similar to that of a clinical psychologist, though usually with less emphasis on research and serious psychopathology is referred to as a counseling psychologist.
Acquisition	Acquisition is the process of adapting to the environment, learning or becoming conditioned. In classical conditoning terms, it is the initial learning of the stimulus response link, which involves a neutral stimulus being associated with a unconditioned stimulus and becoming a conditioned stimulus.
Species	Species refers to a reproductively isolated breeding population.
Carl Rogers	Carl Rogers was instrumental in the development of non-directive psychotherapy, also known as "client-centered" psychotherapy. Rogers' basic tenets were unconditional positive regard, genuineness, and empathic understanding, with each demonstrated by the counselor.
Learning	Learning is a relatively permanent change in behavior that results from experience. Thus, to attribute a behavioral change to learning, the change must be relatively permanent and must result from experience.
Masculinity	Masculinity is a culturally determined value reflecting the set of characteristics of maleness.
Femininity	Femininity is the set of characteristics defined by a culture for idealized females.
Humanistic psychology	Humanistic psychology refers to the school of psychology that focuses on the uniqueness of human beings and their capacity for choice, growth, and psychological health.
Research method	The scope of the research method is to produce some new knowledge. This, in principle, can take three main forms: Exploratory research; Constructive research; and Empirical research.
Scientific observation	An empirical investigation that is structured to answer questions about the world is a scientific observation.
Cultural values	The importance and desirability of various objects and activities as defined by people in a given culture are referred to as cultural values.
McClelland	McClelland asserts that human motivation comprises three dominant needs: the need for achievement (N-Ach), the need for power (N-Pow) and the need for affiliation (N-Affil). The subjective importance of each need varies from individual to individual and depends also on an individual's cultural background.
Aristotle	Aristotle can be credited with the development of the first theory of learning. He concluded that ideas were generated in consciousness based on four principlesof association: contiguity, similarity, contrast, and succession. In contrast to Plato, he believed that knowledge derived from sensory experience and was not inherited.
Spinoza	Spinoza was a determinist who held that absolutely everything that happens occurs through the operation of necessity. All behavior is fully determined, freedom being our capacity to know we are determined and to understand why we act as we do.
Intrinsic motivation	Intrinsic motivation causes people to engage in an activity for its own sake. They are subjective factors and include self-determination, curiosity, challenge, effort, and others.
Feedback	Feedback refers to information returned to a person about the effects a response has had.
Attachment	Attachment is the tendency to seek closeness to another person and feel secure when that person is present.

Go to **Cram101.com** for the Practice Tests for this Chapter.

Go to **Cram101.com** for the Practice Tests for this Chapter.
And, **NEVER** highlight a book again!

Individualism	Individualism refers to putting personal goals ahead of group goals and defining one's identity in terms of personal attributes rather than group memberships.
Individual traits	Personality traits that define a person's unique individual qualities are called individual traits.
Csikszentmihalyi	Csikszentmihalyi is noted for his work in the study of happiness, creativity, subjective well-being, and fun, but is best known for his having been the architect of the notion of flow: "... people are most happy when they are in a state of flow--a Zen-like state of total oneness...".
Wisdom	Wisdom is the ability to make correct judgments and decisions. It is an intangible quality gained through experience. Whether or not something is wise is determined in a pragmatic sense by its popularity, how long it has been around, and its ability to predict against future events.
Altruism	Altruism is being helpful to other people with little or no interest in being rewarded for one's efforts. This is distinct from merely helping others.
Sublimation	Sublimation is a coping mechanism. It refers to rechanneling sexual or aggressive energy into pursuits that society considers acceptable or admirable.
Suppression	Suppression is the defense mechanism where a memory is deliberately forgotten.
Inferiority complex	An inferiority complex is a feeling that one is inferior to others in some way. It is often unconscious, and is thought to drive afflicted individuals to overcompensate, resulting either in spectacular achievement or extreme antisocial behavior.
Attitude	An enduring mental representation of a person, place, or thing that evokes an emotional response and related behavior is called attitude.
Gender role	A cluster of behaviors that characterizes traditional female or male behaviors within a cultural setting is a gender role.

Personality	Personality refers to the pattern of enduring characteristics that differentiates a person, the patterns of behaviors that make each individual unique.
Questionnaire	A self-report method of data collection or clinical assessment method in which the individual being studied checks off items on a printed list, answers multiple-choice questions, or writes out answers to essay questions aimed at producing a selfdescription is called questionnaire.
Self-concept	Self-concept refers to domain-specific evaluations of the self where a domain may be academics, athletics, etc.
Theories	Theories are logically self-consistent models or frameworks describing the behavior of a certain natural or social phenomenon. They are broad explanations and predictions concerning phenomena of interest.
Paradigm	Paradigm refers to the set of practices that defines a scientific discipline during a particular period of time. It provides a framework from which to conduct research, it ensures that a certain range of phenomena, those on which the paradigm focuses, are explored thoroughly. Itmay also blind scientists to other, perhaps more fruitful, ways of dealing with their subject matter.
Kuhn	Kuhn is most famous for his book The Structure of Scientific Revolutions in which he presented the idea that science does not evolve gradually toward truth, but instead undergoes periodic revolutions which he calls "paradigm shifts."
Humanistic perspective	The approach that suggests that all individuals naturally strive to grow, develop, and be in control of their lives and behavior is called the humanistic perspective.
Cognitive behaviorism	Cognitive behaviorism refers to an approach that combines behavioral principles with cognition in order to explain behavior.
Psychoanalytic	Freud's theory that unconscious forces act as determinants of personality is called psychoanalytic theory. The theory is a developmental theory characterized by critical stages of development.
Behaviorism	The school of psychology that defines psychology as the study of observable behavior and studies relationships between stimuli and responses is called behaviorism. Behaviorism relied heavily on animal research and stated the same principles governed the behavior of both nonhumans and humans.
Humanistic	Humanistic refers to any system of thought focused on subjective experience and human problems and potentials.
Learning	Learning is a relatively permanent change in behavior that results from experience. Thus, to attribute a behavioral change to learning, the change must be relatively permanent and must result from experience.
Trait	An enduring personality characteristic that tends to lead to certain behaviors is called a trait. The term trait also means a genetically inherited feature of an organism.
Stages	Stages represent relatively discrete periods of time in which functioning is qualitatively different from functioning at other periods.
Individual differences	Individual differences psychology studies the ways in which individual people differ in their behavior. This is distinguished from other aspects of psychology in that although psychology is ostensibly a study of individuals, modern psychologists invariably study groups.
Heredity	Heredity is the transfer of characteristics from parent to offspring through their genes.
Mischel	Mischel is known for his cognitive social learning model of personality that focuses on the specific cognitive variables that mediate the manner in which new experiences affect the

Go to Cram101.com for the Practice Tests for this Chapter.

individual.

Brain	The brain controls and coordinates most movement, behavior and homeostatic body functions such as heartbeat, blood pressure, fluid balance and body temperature. Functions of the brain are responsible for cognition, emotion, memory, motor learning and other sorts of learning. The brain is primarily made up of two types of cells: glia and neurons.
Neuroticism	Eysenck's use of the term neuroticism (or Emotional Stability) was proposed as the dimension describing individual differences in the predisposition towards neurotic disorder.
Construct	A generalized concept, such as anxiety or gravity, is a construct.
Genetics	Genetics is the science of genes, heredity, and the variation of organisms.
Temperament	Temperament refers to a basic, innate disposition to change behavior. The activity level is an important dimension of temperament.
Insight	Insight refers to a sudden awareness of the relationships among various elements that had previously appeared to be independent of one another.
Self-reflection	In Bandura's social cognitive theory, the ability to analyze one's thoughts and actions is referred to as self-reflection.
Cognitive learning	Higher-level learning involving thinking, knowing, understanding, and anticipation is cognitive learning.
Individual traits	Personality traits that define a person's unique individual qualities are called individual traits.
Self-efficacy	Self-efficacy is the belief that one has the capabilities to execute the courses of actions required to manage prospective situations.
Psychoanalysis	Psychoanalysis refers to the school of psychology that emphasizes the importance of unconscious motives and conflicts as determinants of human behavior. It was Freud's method of exploring human personality.
Humanistic theories	Humanistic theories focus attention on the whole, unique person, especially on the person's conscious understanding of his or her self and the world.
Psychological test	Psychological test refers to a standardized measure of a sample of a person's behavior.
Empirical	Empirical means the use of working hypotheses which are capable of being disproved using observation or experiment.
Psychosis	Psychosis is a generic term for mental states in which the components of rational thought and perception are severely impaired. Persons experiencing a psychosis may experience hallucinations, hold paranoid or delusional beliefs, demonstrate personality changes and exhibit disorganized thinking. This is usually accompanied by features such as a lack of insight into the unusual or bizarre nature of their behavior, difficulties with social interaction and impairments in carrying out the activities of daily living.
Neurosis	Neurosis, any mental disorder that, although may cause distress, does not interfere with rational thought or the persons' ability to function.
Maladjustment	Maladjustment is the condition of being unable to adapt properly to your environment with resulting emotional instability.
Attention	Attention is the cognitive process of selectively concentrating on one thing while ignoring other things. Psychologists have labeled three types of attention: sustained attention, selective attention, and divided attention.

Go to **Cram101.com** for the Practice Tests for this Chapter.

Go to **Cram101.com** for the Practice Tests for this Chapter.
And, **NEVER** highlight a book again!

Intrapsychic conflict	In psychoanalysis, the struggles among the id, ego, and superego are an intrapsychic conflict.
Maladaptive	In psychology, a behavior or trait is adaptive when it helps an individual adjust and function well within their social environment. A maladaptive behavior or trait is counterproductive to the individual.
Psyche	Psyche is the soul, spirit, or mind as distinguished from the body. In psychoanalytic theory, it is the totality of the id, ego, and superego, including both conscious and unconscious components.
Jung	Jung was in some aspects a response to Sigmund Freud's psychoanalysis. He proposed and developed the concepts of the extroverted and introverted personality, archetypes, and the collective unconscious. His work has been influential in psychiatry and in the study of religion, literature, and related fields.
Ego	In Freud's view the Ego serves to balance our primitive needs and our moral beliefs and taboos. Relying on experience, a healthy Ego provides the ability to adapt to reality and interact with the outside world.
Prejudice	Prejudice in general, implies coming to a judgment on the subject before learning where the preponderance of the evidence actually lies, or formation of a judgement without direct experience.
Allport	Allport was a trait theorist. Those traits he believed to predominate a person's personality were called central traits. Traits such that one could be indentifed by the trait, were referred to as cardinal traits. Central traits and cardinal traits are influenced by environmental factors.
Society	The social sciences use the term society to mean a group of people that form a semi-closed (or semi-open) social system, in which most interactions are with other individuals belonging to the group.
Adler	Adler argued that human personality could be explained teleologically, separate strands dominated by the guiding purpose of the individual's unconscious self ideal to convert feelings of inferiority to superiority (or rather completeness). The desires of the self ideal were countered by social and ethical demands.
Cultural values	The importance and desirability of various objects and activities as defined by people in a given culture are referred to as cultural values.
Consciousness	The awareness of the sensations, thoughts, and feelings being experienced at a given moment is called consciousness.
Client-Centered Therapy	Client-Centered Therapy was developed by Carl Rogers. It is based on the principal of talking therapy and is a non-directive approach. The therapist encourages the patient to express their feelings and does not suggest how the person might wish to change, but by listening and then mirroring back what the patient reveals to them, helps them to explore and understand their feelings for themselves.
Encounter group	A type of group that fosters self-awareness by focusing on how group members relate to one another in a setting that encourages open expression of feelings is called an encounter group.
Discrimination	In Learning theory, discrimination refers the ability to distinguish between a conditioned stimulus and other stimuli. It can be brought about by extensive training or differential reinforcement. In social terms, it is the denial of privileges to a person or a group on the basis of prejudice.
Reinforcement	In operant conditioning, reinforcement is any change in an environment that (a) occurs after

Go to **Cram101.com** for the Practice Tests for this Chapter.

the behavior, (b) seems to make that behavior re-occur more often in the future and (c) that reoccurence of behavior must be the result of the change.

Variable	A variable refers to a measurable factor, characteristic, or attribute of an individual or a system.
Bandura	Bandura is best known for his work on social learning theory or Social Cognitivism. His famous Bobo doll experiment illustrated that people learn from observing others.
Collective unconscious	Collective unconscious is a term of analytical psychology, originally coined by Carl Jung. It refers to that part of a person's unconscious which is common to all human beings. It contains archetypes, which are forms or symbols that are manifested by all people in all cultures.
Cognition	The intellectual processes through which information is obtained, transformed, stored, retrieved, and otherwise used is cognition.
Maslow	Maslow is mostly noted today for his proposal of a hierarchy of human needs which he often presented as a pyramid. Maslow was an instrumental player in the formation of the humanistic movement, also known as the third force in psychology.
Sensation	Sensation is the first stage in the chain of biochemical and neurologic events that begins with the impinging of a stimulus upon the receptor cells of a sensory organ, which then leads to perception, the mental state that is reflected in statements like "I see a uniformly blue wall."
Intuition	Quick, impulsive thought that does not make use of formal logic or clear reasoning is referred to as intuition.
Adaptation	Adaptation is a lowering of sensitivity to a stimulus following prolonged exposure to that stimulus. Behavioral adaptations are special ways a particular organism behaves to survive in its natural habitat.
Emotion	An emotion is a mental states that arise spontaneously, rather than through conscious effort. They are often accompanied by physiological changes.
Personality test	A personality test aims to describe aspects of a person's character that remain stable across situations.
Social role	Social role refers to expected behavior patterns associated with particular social positions.
Psychoanalyst	A psychoanalyst is a specially trained therapist who attempts to treat the individual by uncovering and revealing to the individual otherwise subconscious factors that are contributing to some undesirable behavior.
Social psychology	Social psychology is the study of the nature and causes of human social behavior, with an emphasis on how people think towards each other and how they relate to each other.
Individualistic	Cultures have been classified as individualistic, which means having a set of values that give priority to personal goals rather than group goals.
Socioeconomic	Socioeconomic pertains to the study of the social and economic impacts of any product or service offering, market intervention or other activity on an economy as a whole and on the companies, organization and individuals who are its main economic actors.
Neurotransmitter	A neurotransmitter is a chemical that is used to relay, amplify and modulate electrical signals between a neurons and another cell.
Neuroscience	A field that combines the work of psychologists, biologists, biochemists, medical researchers, and others in the study of the structure and function of the nervous system is neuroscience.

Go to Cram101.com for the Practice Tests for this Chapter.

Motives	Needs or desires that energize and direct behavior toward a goal are motives.
Libido	Sigmund Freud suggested that libido is the instinctual energy or force that can come into conflict with the conventions of civilized behavior. Jung, condidered the libido as the free creative, or psychic, energy an individual has to put toward personal development, or individuation.
Developmental psychologist	A psychologist interested in human growth and development from conception until death is referred to as a developmental psychologist.
Affect	A subjective feeling or emotional tone often accompanied by bodily expressions noticeable to others is called affect.
Kagan	The work of Kagan supports the concept of an inborn, biologically based temperamental predisposition to severe anxiety.
Goodness of Fit	With respect to care giving, the degree to which parents and children have compatible temperaments is called goodness of fit.
Child development	Scientific study of the processes of change from conception through adolescence is called child development.
Unconditional positive regard	Unqualified caring and nonjudgmental acceptance of another is called unconditional positive regard.
Adaptive behavior	An adaptive behavior increases the probability of the individual or organism to survive or exist within its environment.
Modeling	A type of behavior learned through observation of others demonstrating the same behavior is modeling.
Adolescence	The period of life bounded by puberty and the assumption of adult responsibilities is adolescence.
Anxiety	Anxiety is a complex combination of the feeling of fear, apprehension and worry often accompanied by physical sensations such as palpitations, chest pain and/or shortness of breath.
Relearning	Relearning refers to a measure of retention used in experiments on memory. Material is usually relearned more quickly than it is learned initially.
Social learning	Social learning is learning that occurs as a function of observing, retaining and replicating behavior observed in others. Although social learning can occur at any stage in life, it is thought to be particularly important during childhood, particularly as authority becomes important.
Reciprocal Determinism	Bandura's term for the social-cognitive view that people influence their environment just as their environment influences them is reciprocal determinism.
Determinism	Determinism is the philosophical proposition that every event, including human cognition and action, is causally determined by an unbroken chain of prior occurrences.
Pluralism	Pluralism refers to the coexistence of distinct ethnic and cultural groups in the same society. Individuals with a pluralistic stance usually advocate that cultural differences be maintained and appreciated.
Individual psychology	Alfred Adler's individual psychology approach views people as motivated by purposes and goals, being creators of their own lives .
Cognitive theories	Cognitive theories emphasize thinking, reasoning, problem solving, and language. Contributions include an emphasis on the active construction of understanding and developmental changes in thinking. Criticisms include giving too little attention to

Go to **Cram101.com** for the Practice Tests for this Chapter.

245

individual variations and underrating the unconscious aspects of thought.

Psychodynamic	Most psychodynamic approaches are centered around the idea of a maladapted function developed early in life (usually childhood) which are at least in part unconscious. This maladapted function (a.k.a. defense mechanism) does not do well in place of a normal/healthy one.
Attitude	An enduring mental representation of a person, place, or thing that evokes an emotional response and related behavior is called attitude.
Self-actualization	Self-actualization (a term originated by Kurt Goldstein) is the instinctual need of a human to make the most of their unique abilities. Maslow described it as follows: Self Actualization is the intrinsic growth of what is already in the organism, or more accurately, of what the organism is.
Motivation	In psychology, motivation is the driving force (desire) behind all actions of an organism.
Metaphor	A metaphor is a rhetorical trope where a comparison is made between two seemingly unrelated subjects
Unstated assumption	Unstated assumption is a type of propaganda message which foregoes explicitly communicating the propaganda's purpose and instead states ideas derived from it. This technique is used when a propaganda's main idea lacks credibility.
Archetype	The archetype is a concept of psychologist Carl Jung. They are innate prototypes for ideas, which may subsequently become involved in the interpretation of observed phenomena. A group of memories and interpretations closely associated with an archetype is called a complex.
Elaboration	The extensiveness of processing at any given level of memory is called elaboration. The use of elaboration changes developmentally. Adolescents are more likely to use elaboration spontaneously than children.
Hypothesis	A specific statement about behavior or mental processes that is testable through research is a hypothesis.
Skinner	Skinner conducted research on shaping behavior through positive and negative reinforcement, and demonstrated operant conditioning, a technique which he developed in contrast with classical conditioning.
Animism	Animism is the belief that inanimate objects have lifelike qualities, are capable of action, and possibly thought.
Mechanistic model	The mechanistic model views development as a passive, predictable response to stimuli.
Superego	Frued's third psychic structure, which functions as a moral guardian and sets forth high standards for behavior is the superego.
Nurture	Nurture refers to the environmental influences on behavior due to nutrition, culture, socioeconomic status, and learning.
Information processing	Information processing is an approach to the goal of understanding human thinking. The essence of the approach is to see cognition as being essentially computational in nature, with mind being the software and the brain being the hardware.
Cognitive approach	A cognitive approach focuses on the mental processes involved in knowing: how we direct our attention, perceive, remember, think, and solve problems.
Subjective experience	Subjective experience refers to reality as it is perceived and interpreted, not as it exists objectively.
Sperry	Sperry separated the corpus callosum, the area of the brain used to transfer signals between the right and left hemispheres, to treat epileptics. He then tested these patients with tasks

that were known to be dependant on specific hemispheres of the brain and demonstrated that the two halves of the brain now had independent functions.

Role-playing

Role-playing refers to a technique that teaches people to behave in a certain way by encouraging them to pretend that they are in a particular situation; it helps people acquire complex behaviors in an efficient way.

George Kelly

George Kelly developed his major contribution to the psychology of personality, The Psychology of Personal Constructs in 1955 and achieved immediate international recognition. He worked in clinical school psychology, developing a program of traveling clinics which also served as a training ground for his students.

Operational definition

An operational definition is the definition of a concept or action in terms of the observable and repeatable process, procedures, and appartaus that illustrates the concept or action.

Scientific method

Psychologists gather data in order to describe, understand, predict, and control behavior. Scientific method refers to an approach that can be used to discover accurate information. It includes these steps: understand the problem, collect data, draw conclusions, and revise research conclusions.

Cognitive-experiential self-theory

Cognitive-experiential self-theory suggests that our efforts to understand the world around us involve two distinct modes of thought: intuitive thought and deliberate, rational thought.

Mental processes

The thoughts, feelings, and motives that each of us experiences privately but that cannot be observed directly are called mental processes.

Teleology

While science investigates natural laws and phenomena, Philosophical naturalism and teleology investigate the existence or non-existence of an organizing principle behind those natural laws and phenomena. Philosophical naturalism asserts that there are no such principles. Teleology asserts that there are.

Aristotle

Aristotle can be credited with the development of the first theory of learning. He concluded that ideas were generated in consciousness based on four principlesof association: contiguity, similarity, contrast, and succession. In contrast to Plato, he believed that knowledge derived from sensory experience and was not inherited.

Free will

The idea that human beings are capable of freely making choices or decisions is free will.

Go to **Cram101.com** for the Practice Tests for this Chapter.

Go to **Cram101.com** for the Practice Tests for this Chapter.
And, **NEVER** highlight a book again!

Printed in the United States
59779LVS00005B/111-112